How to Plan Your Trip to Europe

How to Plan Your Trip to Europe

A Workbook for Independent Travelers

Karen and Ray Gilden

Artha Press

Artha Press, P.O. Box 82722, Portland, Oregon 97282-2722
Copyright © 1995 by Karen Gilden and Ray Gilden

All rights reserved. No part of this book may be reproduced or transmitted in any form or by any means, electronic or mechanical, including photocopying, recording, or by information storage and retrieval system or data base, except as may be expressly permitted by the 1976 Copyright Act or in writing from the publisher. For information address Artha Press, P.O. Box 82722, Portland, Oregon 97282-2722.

Design by Rick Phillips Design, Portland, Oregon
Photography by Ray Gilden
Copyediting by Nadine Fiedler

Printed and bound by Network Graphics, Portland, Oregon
Manufactured in the United States of America
First Printing 1995

ISBN: 1-886922-18-7

Disclaimer of Responsibility

Every effort has been made to make this book as complete and accurate as possible, and we have extensively checked and rechecked facts. Nevertheless, addresses, conditions, and prices change rapidly, and the authors and publisher are not responsible for experiences, conditions, or situations you may encounter that are different from those described.

The companies, organizations, and institutions mentioned in the text are believed to be reliable and reputable. Their inclusion or exclusion in this book is not an endorsement of services or products.

This book may be updated periodically, and the authors would appreciate hearing from you if you find errors, or can provide information that may be helpful to future readers. Please write in care of Artha Press at the above address.

Acknowledgements

We would like to express our sincere thanks to all those who encouraged us in the completion of this book, both before and after the project moved from possibility to reality. Many people read and critiqued the manuscript, and greatly improved it with their comments and suggestions. We also wish to thank the following people, who over the years have not only inspired us, but who made our travels both possible and pleasurable: John and Carolyn Batch, Jan and Ineka Dorland, Thelma Hinshaw, Marybeth and Jerry Medler, Gail Norris, Beverly and Rick Tobias, and especially Jim and Cecile Coffin, who babysat the dog.

Contents

Introduction	1
Step 1—Getting started	3
Some general observations	4
A word about traveling with children	5
Step 2—Collect information	13
National tourist offices	13
Travel books, magazines, and newspapers	14
Other resources	15
When do you need a travel agent?	16
Step 3—Determine how much $$$ you will need	25
Expenses to plan for	28
Money-saving suggestions	29
Foreign currency	32
Credit cards or traveler's checks?	33
Value added tax (VAT)	35
Step 4—Improve your foreign language skills	39
Step 5—Choose your transportation	43
Air travel	43
Rail travel	43
A summary of rail passes in Europe and Britain	45
Car rental, lease, or purchase	48
Driving requirements	50
International Driving Permit	51
Collision damage waiver (CDW)	52
Boat and ferry travel	53
Get a map!	55
Step 6—Choose your accommodations	59
Hotels	59
Youth hostels	60
Apartments	60
Home exchanges	61
Homestays	62
Camping	63
International Camping Carnet	65

Step 7—Order your passport — 69
Visas 70

Step 8—Make your trip a safe one — 77
Thievery and other hassles 77
Protect yourself and your belongings 78
Minimize your vulnerability 78
But what if it happens anyway? 79
A word to women traveling alone 80
Health care 81
Finding medical help 83
Travel insurance 83

Step 9—Start packing — 89
What to take? 90
Typical warm-weather wardrobes 91
Baggage regulations 92
Atlantic transit 93
Arrival 94
What if your bags aren't there
when you are? 95
Staying in touch while in Europe 96
Avoiding jet lag 97

Step 10—Retain your memories — 101
Take a camera 101
Keep a journal 103
Take a micro tape recorder 103
Purchase post cards 103
Souvenirs 103
Coming home 104

Afterword — 107

Resources — 109

Index — 127

Photographs: p. 2—castle in France; p. 6—Venice gondolier; p. 29—library of Celsus in Ephesus, Turkey; p. 34—fishermen in Nazare, Portugal; p. 40—wine shop in Chalabre; p. 44—Trevi fountain in Rome; p. 47—London street scene; p. 54—church on Samos; p. 63—English village shop; p. 64—camping in Salamonca, Spain; p. 71—Spanish Windmills; p. 84—workers in Istanbul; p. 86—Portuguese village woman.

Preface

Everything begins with an idea, which leads to a plan, which becomes reality.

In 1977, as part of a six-month journey, we spent five weeks camping in the Soviet Union. The cold war was raging, Brezhnev was in power, and Jimmy Carter was talking about neutron bombs. On a hot Moscow afternoon we visited an ill-kept public garden with two new friends, the Russian parents of a young woman we had met in the U.S. The garden was attached to a prerevolutionary mansion, now a run-down museum, and had been chosen for our walk because it was spacious and unoccupied—we could speak freely there. As we strolled the gravel paths we talked about our very different lives, and about the trip we were taking.

"How did such a wonderful thing happen?" we were asked. "How did you manage such a trip?"

"It was just an idea," Ray replied. "But we kept thinking about it, and we started making plans, and here we are."

"You are very lucky," he said. "We could never do such a thing. Here, we can have thousands of ideas—but they all die within us."

Fortunately, things have changed for people living in the former Soviet Union and, for some of them at least, ideas now *can* become reality. But no matter where we live, all of us struggle to achieve our dreams. This workbook is about helping you do what we did—turn your ideas, and your dream of travel, into the real thing.

Introduction

Several years ago a travel agent asked us to teach a series of workshops for clients who wanted to visit Europe on their own and on a budget—people who wanted to avoid rushed and crowded tours, but who felt uncertain about traveling independently. Because we travel that way ourselves, and know from experience the pitfalls and joys of independent budget travel, we agreed.

The classes were popular, and we subsequently taught them several times. This ten-step workbook is a compendium of the ideas and materials used in those classes. It doesn't offer vivid descriptions of romantic holiday resorts, or list 100 "best" restaurants, or 50 of Europe's most affecting sights. In fact, it doesn't say anything about what to see and where to go, because we think you should make your own decisions, based on your own research and your own dreams. What this workbook *will* do is show you how to make informed decisions about your future trip. It will show you how to find the materials you need to make decisions, and it will help you plan a budget, get a passport, convert currency, and travel safely. It is designed to be written in, with pages for your own notes and reminders, and each chapter ends with a to-do list that prompts you to stay focused and on track. If you complete these "to dos"—and save your money—your trip will become a reality.

How can we be sure? Because we've done it. We've visited 23 countries (many of them several times) traveling by train, plane, bus, ferry, and automobile. We've driven over 25,000 miles in Europe, in cars that we've rented, leased, and purchased (new and used). We've stayed in hotels, pensions, campgrounds, private homes, auberges, zimmers, apartments, and a VW bus. We've made mistakes. We've been burglarized, searched, lost, and sick, but we've also seen glorious art and architecture, met wonderful people, formed life-long friendships, and learned more about ourselves in the process than we ever thought possible.

To find time to travel we have quit jobs and taken leaves of absence. We are frugal travelers because our money is limited, but also because we have learned that adventure, fun, and real understanding are to be found more easily in third class than in first. (We subscribe to the adage "the cheaper the trip, the richer the experience.")

We have definite ideas—biases—about traveling, which will no doubt become apparent as you read through the steps. A few, we think, deserve special mention: we believe that a good traveler is one who approaches each trip with an open mind and an open heart—a task much harder than the cliché words would have you believe. This ideal traveler is flexible and process-oriented, accepting each day and event as it comes, knowing that even setbacks can lead to adventure, and enjoying and learning from every experience. A tourist (or vacationer), on the other hand, is goal-oriented. Tourists want—for the most part—to arrive, to relax, and to look, but to remain uninvolved with the life and lives around them. There's nothing wrong with being a tourist—as long as you know what you're doing.

We hope that whether you're a traveler or a tourist, you will take with you a sense of humor, a good deal of patience, and the determination to resist declaring your beliefs and way of life the "correct" ones. (It helps to repeat, like a mantra, the words "different country, different customs," when faced with inexplicable and irritating behavior.)

We also believe good travelers leave things as they find them. Like good wilderness backpackers who remove all signs of their campsite and pack their trash out with them, good travelers don't litter, don't deface any kind of property, and don't carry away "samples" of anything. They do respect time-honored traditions, religious and cultural; they observe and emulate (when possible and appropriate) the society around them, and they offer only legitimate complaints.

Last, we believe planning can never begin too early. There are so many people to talk to, so much to read, so much to learn. And the more you learn the better, because taking one trip abroad usually means you'll take a second and even a third—travel is addictive.

Even if you're just dreaming about far-off places, planning can make that dream come true. When we decided to take our first six-month trip in 1976, we had no savings and no idea how we were going to get time off from our jobs to travel. But because we wanted so much to do it, we set a date. We told friends and relatives we were going. Our daughter, then ten, made an elaborate countdown sheet and together we ritually placed a checkmark in a square at the end of every day. We spoke about our trip only in positive terms: no "ifs" were allowed, only "whens." Every brochure and article we collected, every list made and plan discussed, brought the dream closer. And when the sun finally rose on the date we had optimistically set ten months before, we were ready, because we had made the trip our first priority, and because we had planned.

Step 1—Getting started

Some trips just happen: a friend makes a suggestion, someone else mentions the great time they had in Italy, your travel agent tells you Portugal is inexpensive, and your kids say, well, they guess they can stand to be away from their friends, if you promise they can go to the beach. Before you know it your trip has a shape and substance of its own and the airline tickets are in your hand. Do you really want to do this? Too many people take the trip someone else wants to take, then wonder why they come home disappointed and disillusioned.

Personally, we think *any* reason to travel is a good one, but not everyone agrees. To avoid taking the wrong trip, sit down and think about your own personal "why?." Here are a few ideas to get you started (of course, there are no right or wrong answers):

- Are you going because your spouse or a friend talked you into it?

- Is this trip "just a vacation," or is it a long-anticipated adventure? (In other words, will you be a tourist or a traveler?)

- Will you mix business with pleasure?

- Do you have a goal that your traveling companions may not share? (Do you, for instance, have a secret and unexpressed desire to photograph every pub in northwest England?)

- What do you see yourself doing in Europe? Visiting museums? Enjoying the peace of an isolated Greek isle? Dancing all night in a posh London club? Backpacking through the Pyrenees?

- Are you returning to the land of your ancestors? Do you plan to look up relatives?

Once you acknowledge your own personal why, talk to your fellow travelers about theirs. What do they want to do? How do they want to spend their time? What visions do they see when they daydream about *their* upcoming trip?

It's not unusual to find that traveling companions have made entirely different assumptions about a trip, thinking that if they've agreed on purchasing Eurail passes and on a destination, everything else is settled. We're not saying that art lovers and sun worshippers can't travel together and have a great time—they can. We are suggesting that you talk it over *before* you purchase that expensive, nonrefundable ticket, and then make your plans accordingly. Once you understand the very important *why* you are traveling, you can get down to the business of when, where, and how.

Some general observations

While some travelers have a specific place and purpose in mind when they begin planning, most have only vague dreams that include seeing everything: the famous cities, the famous museums, the famous rivers, the famous castles, beaches, cathedrals, ruins. . . . Decision-making can be tough.

Here are three important issues to keep in mind as you start the planning process:

Weather: Many of the brochures you receive will typify the weather: "warm, sunny days and blissfully cool nights," or, "winter conditions make it perfect for skiing and skating." Such descriptions may depict the average summer or winter, but last year's weather is more reliable, as in, "This rain is really unusual, you should have been here last year." Avoid making plans that require "perfect" weather and you will avoid disappointment.

We can say this about European weather: spring is cooler than fall, summers are generally warm, but not necessarily dry. Winters are cold. The southern countries (Spain, southern France, Italy, Greece, and the Turkish coast) have warm to very-hot summers, so if you melt in hot weather consider north or central Europe. Scandinavia has comfortably warm summers, but cold weather and short days move in early.

Our favorite time for travel is September through November, or April through June. These are "shoulder seasons," and in most places you will find reasonably good weather, lower prices, and fewer tourists. Campgrounds in the north may close after the middle of September, but we've had no problem finding places in southern Europe well into November. If you can only travel during the winter, don't despair: Portugal's Algarve, Morocco, Greece, and southern Spain and southern Turkey are all good options.

Expenses: If you're traveling on a tight budget, where and when you travel can make a big difference. The advent of the European Economic Community (now commonly known as the European Union, or EU) has brought some leveling of prices, but it is still true that the southern countries, especially Spain, Portugal, and Greece, are less expensive than northern ones and that Scandinavian countries are the most expensive. Eastern Europe is still a bargain, and relatively free of tourists away from the cities, but this is rapidly changing.

Time spent in any major city is twice or three times more expensive than time spent in a village or small town.

Traveling off-season is cheaper than traveling in high season. Hotel rates fall; so does the price of an airline ticket. Spring and fall are less pricey than the summer, and careful shopping can often lead to bargain air rates during those months.

Crowds: Unfortunately, all the sites you go to Europe to see are the sites that everyone else goes to Europe to see. Expect crowds, and you won't be disappointed. You can avoid them, however, and still see much that is beautiful, unique, and charming. Back roads, small towns, and unheard-of villages will gain you peace and quiet and a "real life" feeling for Europe. This is true in every country, and more so in eastern Europe. If you hate crowds, shun the French and Italian Riverias, Spain's Costa Del Sol, and most Greek islands during the summer months.

It's also worth knowing that in France, and especially Paris, many small shops and restaurants shut down in August, when almost everyone takes their month-long holiday. It's not the best time to experience true Parisian culture; you're likely to find more Germans and Americans than French.

No matter what your destination, we urge you to consider the loose itinerary, the slower pace, the narrower field of view. We think a loose plan of action—as opposed to a strict itinerary—increases the chances for a successful trip. Europe is full of surprises, even for return visitors. Allow one or two days a week for relaxation, for extending a visit in a place you like, and for duties that take much longer than they do here at home, like finding a post office, buying stamps, finding a phone to call home—and figuring out how to use it.

Tip: *Europe is full of fabulous galleries and museums: the Louvre, the Prado, the British, the Uffizi—to name just a few. Plan to enjoy them but beware of museum exhaustion. Several short visits are better than devoting an entire day. Know when you start out that you won't see everything, and try not to regret what you missed. Save something for your next trip.*

A word about traveling with children

Children, like adults, differ in their tolerance for travel. For some the constant change and new demands are fun, for others they create frustration and fear. Parents, obviously, are the best judge of how their children will meet these challenges. But most children, given the opportunity, are curious, anxious to learn, and highly resilient—all traits that favor the traveler.

Europe is a wonderful place for children to visit. Besides the fairytale castles and ruins that all children love, there are ancient monuments like Stonehenge and the Parthenon that will spark their imagination. Special parks such as Madurodam in Holland and Tivoli Gardens in Copenhagen, as well as uncounted municipal parks, zoos, and playgrounds, can provide hours of fun. There are museums dedicated to children across Europe, and even formal galleries like the Louvre can be fun, if taken in small doses.

Imagine taking your children to the top of the Eiffel Tower, or to explore the cave paintings of central France. Would they like the elaborate fountains of Rome, the crown jewels in the Tower of London, or the gondolas of Venice—all sights unlike anything they can see at home? Our own experience suggests that children love all these things, and are ready and willing to tackle any adventure you can offer. And when you need a break, reliable babysitters can be found through local travel information offices, chambers of commerce, large hotels, and even some department stores.

It's normal to be concerned about issues of cleanliness, food, and health when traveling with children, but most of your worry is, in our opinion, needless. You can take the same precautions in Europe as you do at home, and children are often more flexible and adaptable than their parents. Some

years ago in Venice we met a British family of five (the youngest a six-month-old infant) who were traveling around the world in a pickup style camper. When we next heard from them, 18 months later, they were in the United States after driving through Europe, the Middle East, India, and Australia, and all were healthy and happy.

How old should your children be to travel? Cynthia Harriman, author of *Take Your Kids to Europe,* says children are old enough to travel abroad "when they can carry their own baggage and don't wet the bed or need three changes of clothes a day."

When we began traveling, our daughter was eleven—young enough to willingly adapt to our plans and suggestions; old enough to appreciate and remember what she was seeing. She always traveled with us, until she left home to travel on her own, and her presence gave our trips a dimension they would not otherwise have had. On that first trip we took her out of school for three months and never regretted it. At the age of eleven she discovered a natural talent for languages, a predilection for trying new foods, and an appreciation for other cultures that set her on the road to becoming an anthropologist. Travel may not have quite that effect on your children, but we suspect it will make a positive difference, and we highly recommend it.

To do...

1. Make a list of your reasons for taking this trip, or write down all the things you would like to see and do while traveling. Ask your travel companions to do the same, then talk about how these ideas will influence your planning.

2. Start a notebook. A three-ring binder with pocket dividers works best, but anything will do if it can be organized into sections and has room for the brochures and clippings you'll be collecting. This is where you'll file articles clipped from newspapers or magazines, note the tip on that Paris hotel your sister in-law stayed in, and jot down the best place to buy Czech glassware. A well-organized binder will save you hours of searching for misplaced nuggets of information. As your departure date nears, sort through your material, toss out what you don't need, and transfer the rest to a small, easy-to-carry notebook.

3. Get a large map of Europe (the American Automobile Association has good ones, but any map showing mileage or kilometers will do) and sketch out your dream trip. Now get a calculator and add up the miles. Have you bitten off too much? Begin again.

4. Begin monitoring currency exchange rates, and the temperatures in cities that may be on your itinerary. Your newspaper will probably have them, but if not, check the *New York Times, Wall Street Journal,* or *USA Today.*

5. Design a chart or graph depicting each day that remains until your trip. Post it on your refrigerator or bulletin board, and mark off each day at bedtime. This visual reminder will keep you inspired, and it's fun to watch departure day draw near.

6. How well do you know Europe? Can you fill in the blank map on the following page?

How many European countries can you identify?

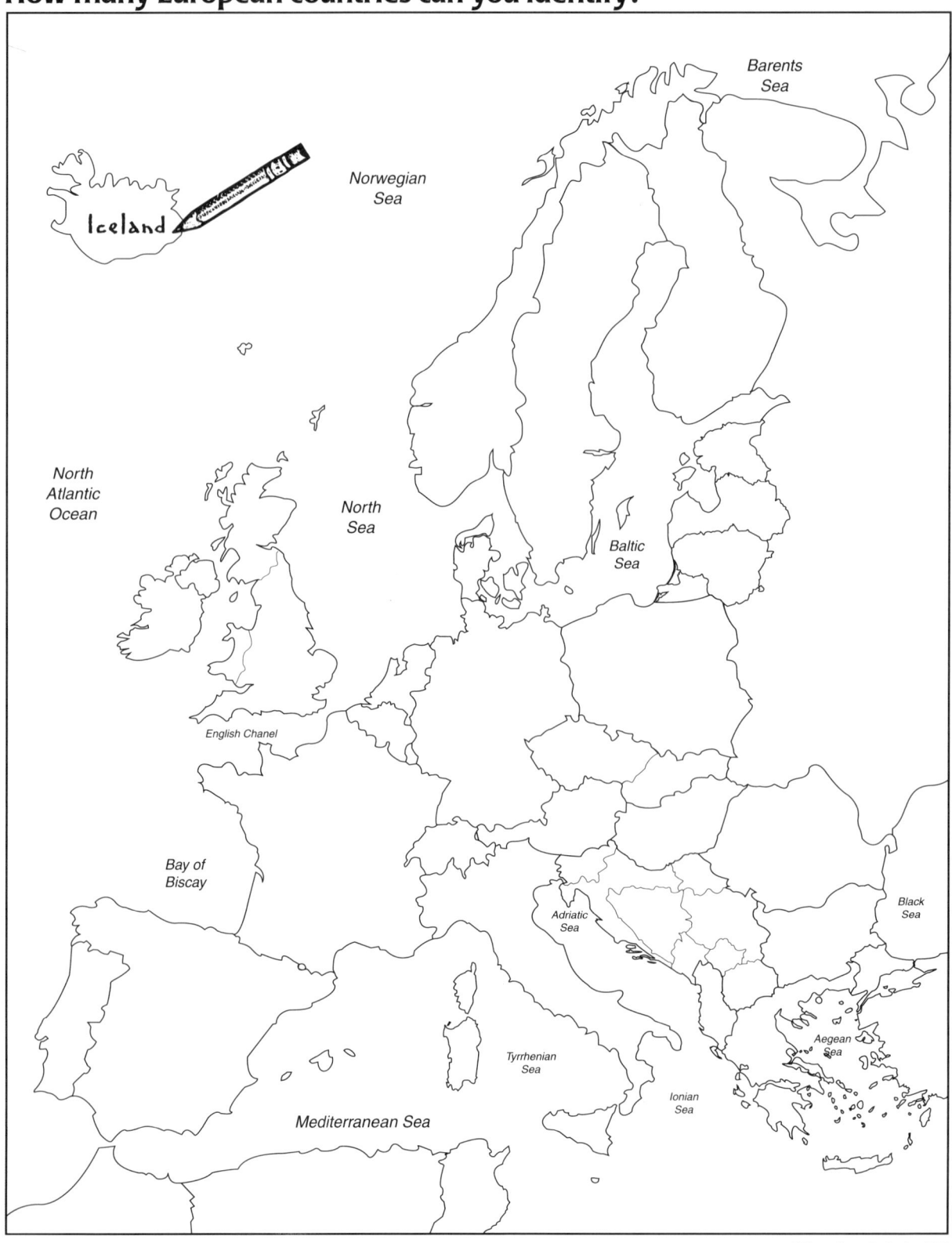

See page 118 in the Resources section for a completed map.

To Europe! A timeline checklist

This list is not inclusive; it provides a timeline for the *kinds* of things that need to be done at certain points in your planning. Use it in addition to the to-do lists that follow each step. We suggest that you tear it out, post it in a visible place, and check off items as you complete them. You might want to photocopy it, so it will be available for a second or third trip. (Not all items will apply to every trip; feel free to ignore those not pertinent to yours.)

Six months or more (if possible)

- ❑ Study a language (at minimum, learn courtesy words and phrases).
- ❑ Purchase a binder or other trip notebook and begin filling it.
- ❑ Start reading everything you can about European history, culture, art, architecture.
- ❑ Order information from national travel offices.
- ❑ Arrange for house or apartment rentals in Europe, if desired.

Five months

- ❑ Write auto companies, rail companies for information.
- ❑ Request government pamphlets.
- ❑ Decide means of transportation while in Europe.
- ❑ Make a general plan (itinerary).
- ❑ Begin to explore home-exchange options, if interested.
- ❑ Inquire about inoculations. Get, if needed.

Three to four months

- ❑ Continue research and reading.
- ❑ Make airline reservations. Join airline mileage club.
- ❑ Order vehicle for purchase or rental, or purchase rail pass.
- ❑ Make hotel reservations for (at least) first and perhaps second day after arrival.
- ❑ Apply for passports and visas, if required.
- ❑ If traveling with a car in peak season, make ferry or Chunnel reservations.

- ❐ If traveling for an extended period of time, arrange for rental of your home/apartment, or for a house sitter.
- ❐ Check to see if your medical insurance covers you in Europe.
- ❐ Call or write to travel insurance companies for information.
- ❐ Check expiration date of driver's license; renew if necessary.
- ❐ If camping, decide what equipment to take and what to buy abroad.

One to two months

- ❐ If your trip is lengthy, consider having an accountant pay your bills while you are gone and/or add a trusted person to your checking account.
- ❐ Purchase any additional clothing (make sure new shoes are thoroughly broken in before takeoff), luggage, camera, film, or other special hobby equipment you plan to take.
- ❐ Apply for international driving permit (page 50) and international camping carnet (page 65), if needed.

Three to four weeks

- ❐ Prepay all insurance policies, mortgage, utilities not to be discontinued.
- ❐ Confirm that auto insurance won't expire while you are away. (Expiration may increase the cost when you take it up again.)
- ❐ Prepare a first-aid kit with your regular (and duplicate) prescriptions, an extra pair of glasses or contacts, and emergency addresses and phone numbers.
- ❐ Plan gifts to take from home for friends and people you encounter. These might include small items with logos from local businesses or a college or university, books or calendars containing photos of your local area, souvenir pins of your state or city, and postcards.
- ❐ Prepare an itinerary with approximate locations and dates so friends and relatives at home can get in touch with you if necessary.
- ❐ Arrange for auto storage, if applicable.

One to two weeks

- ❐ Make money arrangements: buy traveler's checks and record numbers in your take-along notebook; pack a small calculator for currency conversion.

- ❐ Order foreign currency from your local bank.
- ❐ Arrange for mail pickup and discontinuation of newspapers, garbage.
- ❐ Arrange for care of lawn, pets, plants.
- ❐ Test-pack, eliminating about half of what you'd planned to take.

One to two days

- ❐ Give duplicate keys for house/car to neighbor.
- ❐ Confirm hotel, ferry, plane (and seat) reservations.
- ❐ Pack, remembering that everything will be carried by you.
- ❐ Store valuables. Store outdoor equipment (yard tools, etc.) in a garage or other safe place.

Day of departure

Make sure you have:
- ❐ Tickets, passports.
- ❐ Cash, traveler's checks, savings account numbers, credit cards, PIN numbers, telephone calling card, checkbook.
- ❐ Immunization record if needed.
- ❐ Travel notebook, maps, guidebooks.
- ❐ Camping carnet, international driver's license.
- ❐ Addresses and phone numbers you may need here and abroad.
- ❐ Photocopies of all important documents.

Make sure you do:
- ❐ Turn on automatic timer for lights. Adjust thermostat. Turn off hot water heater.
- ❐ Lock all windows and doors and disconnect electrical appliances, such as coffee makers.
- ❐ Count your pieces of luggage, including purses and camera bags. *Each time you move them, count them again.*

Notes

Step 2—Collect information

This is the easiest part of the planning process, and the most fun. The only hard part is choosing from all the available sources: books, magazines, newsletters, brochures, computer resources, travel agents, television shows, videos, and more. Like everything else in the information age, travel knowledge is sold, listed, documented, indexed, and given away in exponentially increasing amounts. Once you start looking, you'll find more than you want to know; the trick is to stay on track and use only what you need.

Even if you have a clear idea of where, when, and how your trip will unfold, don't restrict your search to details. If that sounds contradictory, given the admonition to stay on track, remember that there is a natural progression to fact-gathering. If you begin slowly and cast a wide net, the details and logistics will become clearer and easier to resolve as your base of knowledge grows. Especially if you have a year or more to plan, spend time collecting brochures, studying guidebooks, and reading history (daydreaming is also a good idea). You can stay on track while discovering unknown treasures along the way.

Once your search begins in earnest, don't be surprised to find yourself taking a proprietary interest in the country(s) of your choice. That interest will continue long after you've returned home. Frequent travelers who do their homework usually become addicted to their subject. They become citizens of the world, at least in spirit.

Here is a list of resources from which to draw—you'll undoubtedly find others. If you haven't started a trip notebook, now is the time to do so.

National tourist offices

For the price of a postcard or a one-minute phone call, national tourist offices will send you lots of colorful and informative brochures. While the quality of publications and staffing varies, we have found these offices to be good resources and an excellent starting point for your research. Some can and will provide maps, railroad timetables, camping information, hotel ratings, and special-events calendars—all free. (A few offices, like Great Britain's, offer additional publications available for purchase.)

If you have questions about an area or an activity (for example, skiing facilities, music festivals, or campgrounds), just ask. In most cases, you'll get the answer you need. Write or call them early and expect to wait about a month

Tip: *Always ask for a list of events when writing to national tourist offices. They're a great aid in planning, if your interests lie in that direction, and if you want to shun crowds, you'll know which places to avoid, and when.*

for a reply. Calling, of course, is faster and faxing is best, as it saves time spent on hold, especially during the busy summer months.

Keep in mind that the colorful brochures flooding your mailbox are designed to inspire you to visit—not everything is as picture-perfect as the brochures would have you believe. Note, for instance, the marked lack of crowds and other distractions in the photos of famous sites—not real life, we're sorry to report.

Travel books, magazines, and newspapers

Travel books are a blessing and a curse. There are so many, how can one choose? There are guidebooks telling you where to go and what to see; there are specialty travel books for walkers, drivers, trekkers, sailors, and bicyclers; there are books for wine tasters and gourmets, bibliophiles and history buffs, art lovers and pub crawlers. There are how-to-do-it books, like this one; there are books for armchair travelers—tales of adventure and romance in faraway places; and there are combinations of all these. How to decide? The only way is just to dig in.

- Use your public library and your librarian. He or she can help you find all kinds of books about the countries you'll be visiting, and it's free. So go there first and start reading everything you can get your hands on—geography, history, politics, social commentary. And don't forget fiction by native authors.

- Good how-to guidebooks offer pertinent, up-to-the minute advice, and even experienced travelers find them worth a look. Some, like *Let's Go, Lonely Planet, Berkeley Guides,* and *Europe Through the Back Door* appeal primarily to budget travelers. Others, like *Fodor's, Fielding's,* and *Frommer's,* usually include some moderate and high-priced establishments in their selections. Make sure your guidebook is the most current available (check the copyright date), and don't assume that your taste and expectations will necessarily agree with the author's.

(Two of these guidebooks now offer fax updates of their guides for a small fee. For information about Fodor's World View Travel Update call 800-799-9609. To reach Fielding's City Fax—information sheets on London and Paris—call 800-635-9777.)

- General guide books, the kind that rank sites and provide historical background, are nice to have along, but our experience is that they often get shoved in the suitcase and forgotten while we're off exploring things the books forgot to mention. It is nice, however, to have some kind of general guide along with you. We like *Michelin Green Guides,* which are dependable, a handy size, and can be found all over Europe and in good travel bookstores in the U.S. *Baedecker's* and *Blue Guides* are also good, if a bit dry. Once in Europe you will find plenty of site-specific guidebooks, like *A Day in Toledo* or *A Day in Florence.* The English is often quaint, they are not terribly thorough, and they can be expensive, but they're helpful.

- Specialized books are also plentiful. Whether your interest is the London of Sherlock Holmes, the Paris of the French Impressionists, or early Christian Rome, if you look, chances are you will find a guidebook designed just for you.

The down side to all this plentitude is that books are heavy and take up valuable space. So read as much as you can before you leave home, then photocopy the pages you need, or transfer the information to your handy notebook. Or, if you can bring yourself to do it, tear out the sections you want to take along.

- Many travel magazines cater to upscale travelers, giving the mistaken impression that you can only afford Europe if you have more than $500 a day. This is not true, but don't give up on the magazines. They do print wonderful, inspiring photographs, entertaining articles (sometimes), and occasionally useful information. Glean as much as you can, and discount the elitism inherent in the rest. (Condé Nast *Traveler* is one of the best—their "Stop Press" section contains valuable late-breaking information, and their ombudsman column has been helpful to many—and is a good source for travel tips.) Two magazines focusing on budget and independent travel are *International Travel News,* full of first-person accounts and useful advertising, and *Affordable Travel,* due out in June, 1995. There are also magazines such as *EcoTraveler* that emphasize, well, ecotravel.

- City newspapers with lengthy travel sections are good sources for current prices, exchange rates, weather, and up-to-the-minute tips on restaurants, hotels, and sights. (Note: exchange rates listed in the business sections of newspapers are usually bank wholesale rates. They are *not* the rates you will receive when changing money.)

Other resources

Culturegrams are issued by Brigham Young University's Kennedy Center for International Studies. They provide a concise look at a country's history, customs, and culture, including topics of special interest to travelers, such as eating and diet, courtesies, transportation, and health. *Culturegrams* are like Cliff notes—minicourses in a country's people and their customs where you can pick up tidbits like "Etiquette is important [in France] . . . Lettuce is folded into small pieces with the fork but never cut." And, "It is improper to help oneself twice to cheese."

Culturegrams are $3 each for up to five countries ($1.50 each for six to 19 countries, and $1 each for 20–49 countries). To request an order form, send a stamped, self-addressed envelope to Brigham Young University, Kennedy Center Publications, P.O. Box 24538, Provo, UT 84602-4538. You can call 801-378-6528 to order with a credit card.

A number of bookstores specialize in travel books, and some offer catalog sales. They are listed on page 18 and in Resources.

Travel newsletters are popular and generally more focused than general interest magazines. There are many to choose from; a selection is given in Resources.

Travel videos can be obtained from public libraries, travel stores, video rental outlets and from travel agents. (Don't let videos substitute for the real thing.)

Computer resources, such as Compuserve, Prodigy, America Online, and Usenet groups, offer travel information. If you have a computer and a modem, you may also be able to hook directly into your public library or local college library. Some specific travel-related Internet addresses are listed in Resources.

The U.S. Government publishes useful and definitive brochures, and most are free. Among these are *Know Before You Go, Buyer Beware,* and *Tips for Travelers.* Write to U.S. Customs Service Publications, 1301 Constitution Avenue, N.W., Washington, DC 20229.

The Superintendent of Documents, U.S. Government Printing Office, Washington, D.C. 20402; Tel. 202-512-1800, can supply you with *Health Information for International Travelers* ($7), *Camper's First Aid* ($2.50), *Travel Tips for Older Americans, Visa Requirements for Foreign Governments,* and *Your Trip Abroad.*

When do you need a travel agent?

Mr. Jones goes into his neighborhood travel agency, sits down at Ms. Smith's desk, and says he wants to go to Europe.

"Where in Europe?" says Smith, politely.

"Well," says Jones, settling comfortably into his chair, "I haven't decided. Wherever it's most interesting, I guess."

"Well," says Smith, "what would you like to see?"

"Oh, you know," says Jones, "all the usual things."

"When do you want to go?" she inquires.

"When do you suggest?" he replies.

"What kind of budget do you have in mind?"

"How much is it going to cost?"

Enough! You can see that neither party is making headway. Smith is getting frustrated as she sees waiting customers depart, and callers put on hold. Jones isn't learning anything and will be lucky if his trip gets off the ground.

You, however, know what you need. You call several travel agents, give your destination and time frame for travel, and ask for sample fares. You inquire what other services the agency offers that you might use: Do they sell Eurail or other train passes, book rental cars, hotels, ferries? Do they sell travel insurance? Will they send you the relevant information?

Now you can study the brochures at your leisure, compare them with similar material you've sought out for yourself, and, when ready, call the agent to make your reservations and purchase your tickets. You and the agent have both benefited, with no loss of time and no frustration.

Travel agents do not charge for their services, and a good one can be an asset and will save you money. A bad one, on the other hand, can cost you money and even mislead you. Deregulation has forced agencies to become more creatively competitive, and those that succeed are doing so because they offer better service or cheaper fares. Unfortunately, agents make most of their money selling packaged tours, and there are few incentives to work with independent travelers who require lots of time, help, and advice, but who seldom purchase more than an airline ticket.

Are there agents in your town who specialize in independent travel? If so, they are worth a visit. A knowledgeable agent can offer suggestions and money-saving tips that might take you hours of research. But don't be a Mr. Jones. Before your visit, make sure you know what you need. If you've done your research, you probably know more than the travel agent.

Step 2/ to do ...

___ 1 Write or call the national tourist offices of countries you may visit, and request information (list begins on page 20).

___ 2 Visit your library and local bookstore for books about your destination. Don't forget the travel sections of newspapers from other cities, and back issues of travel magazines.

___ 3 Write to the U.S. Customs Service Publications, 1301 Constitution Ave., Washington, D.C. 20229, for the following brochures:

    Know Before You Go ___   *Buyer Beware* ___
    Tips for Travelers ___   *Your Trip Abroad* ___

___ 4 Request catalogs from these sources (more resources are listed in the appendix):
    Brigham Young University *Culturegrams*
    Kennedy Center Publications
    P. O. Box 24538
    Provo, UT 84602-4538

    Forsyth Travel Library (books, maps, more)
    9154 W. 57th Street (P.O. Box 2975)
    Shawnee Mission, KS 66201-1375 (Tel. 800-367-7984)

    Magellan's (luggage, travel accessories, gifts)
    P.O. Box 5485
    Santa Barbara, CA 93150-5485 (Tel. 800-962-4943)

    Traveller's Bookstore (books, maps, more)
    22 West 52nd Street
    New York, NY 10019 (Tel. 212-664-0995)

___ 5 If you subscribe to Compuserve, America Online, or others, check out their travel resources. If you have access to Usenet news groups, read "rec.travel.misc," "rec.travel.europe," "rec.travel.marketplace," or "rec.travel.air."

___ 6 Don't forget to save pertinent information in your notebook. Make it work as your personal travel guide.

___ 7 Have you decided which countries you will visit? If so, test your knowledge with the quiz on the next page.

A quick quiz

You'll have a head start on understanding the people and the cultures of places you visit if you can answer these basic questions. (We guarantee that all but the most isolated individual will know this much or more about the U.S.)

1. Where is the country you are visiting, in relation to other European countries? (Who are its neighbors?)

2. What is its capital city?

3. What system of government does it have? How long has it been in place?

4. Is the current ruling party right, left, center, or somewhere else?

5. Is there a state-supported or predominant religion?

6. If yes, what religion is it?

7. Are U.S. soldiers stationed in the country? (Don't be surprised to find yourself in a discussion about the value or detriment of this.)

8. What are the country's major crops or industries?

9. Name two events in the country's history widely believed to be most important.

National tourist offices

Andorra Tourism
6800 N. Knox Avenue
Lincolnwood, IL 60646
Tel. 708-674-3091
Date ordered _____
❒ Received

Austrian National Tourist Office
P.O. Box 90049
Los Angeles, CA 90049
Tel. 310-477-3332
Fax 310-477-5141
Date ordered _____
❒ Received

Belgian Tourist Office
780 Third Avenue
New York, NY 10017
Tel. 212-758-8130
Fax 212-355-7675
Date ordered _____
❒ Received

British Tourist Authority
(England, Scotland, Wales, and Northern Ireland)
551 Fifth Avenue
New York, NY 10176
Tel. 212-986-2200
Fax 212-986-1188
Date ordered _____
❒ Received

Bulgarian National Tourist Agency
317 Madison Avenue, Suite 508
New York, NY 10017
Tel. 212-573-5530
Fax 212-573-5538
Date ordered _____
❒ Received

Czech Republic: Cedok Central European Travel
10 East 40th Street, #3604
New York, NY 10016
Tel. 212-689-9720
Fax 212-481-0597
Date ordered _____
❒ Received

Danish Tourist Board
[See Scandinavia]

Estonian Consulate
630 Fifth Avenue, Suite 2415
New York, NY 10111
Tel. 212-247-0499
Fax 212-262-0893
Date ordered _____
❒ Received

Finnish Tourist Board
(See Scandinavia)

French Govt. Tourist Office
444 Madison Avenue
New York, NY 10022
Tel. 212-838-7800
Info: 900-990-0040 (50¢ per minute)
Fax 212-838-7855
Date ordered _____
❒ Received

German National Tourist Office
122 East 42nd Street
New York, NY 10168
Tel. 212-661-7200
Date ordered _____
❒ Received

Tip: Most government tourist offices are on the East Coast. Calling before 8 a.m. from the West Coast will get you the lowest telephone rate. It's best to call or fax, because these addresses seem to change frequently, and your written request may be delayed as a result.

Gibraltar Information Bureau
1155 15th Street NW, Suite 710
Washington, DC 20005
Tel. 202-452-1108
Fax 202-872-8543
Date ordered _____
❐ Received

Greek National Tourist Office
645 Fifth Avenue, Olympic Tower
New York, NY 10022
Tel. 212-421-5777
Date ordered _____
❐ Received

Hungary
No tourisim office. Write or call the
Hungarian Embassy
3910 Shoemaker Street, N.W.
Washington, D.C. 20008
Tel. 202-362-6730
Date ordered _____
❐ Received

Icelandic Tourist Board
(See Scandinavia)

Irish Tourist Board
(not *Northern Ireland*)
345 Park Avenue
New York, NY 10154
Tel. 212-418-0800
or toll-free 800-223-6470
Fax 212-371-9052
Date ordered _____
❐ Received

Italian Govt. Travel Office
630 Fifth Avenue, Suite 1565
New York, NY 10111
Tel. 212-245-4822
Fax 212-586-9249
Date ordered _____
❐ Received

Latvian Embassy
4325 17th Street
Washington, D.C. 20011
Tel. 202-726-8213
Date ordered _____
❐ Received

Lithuanian Embassy
2622 16th Street
Washington, D.C. 20009
Tel. 202-234-5860
Date ordered _____
❐ Received

Luxembourg National Tourist Office
17 Beekman Place
New York, NY 10022
Tel. 212-935-8888
Fax 212-935-5896
Date ordered _____
❐ Received

Malta National Tourist Office
350 Fifth Avenue, Suite 4412
New York, NY 10118
Tel. 212-695-9520
Fax 212-695-8229
Date ordered _____
❐ Received

Monaco Govt. Tourist Bureau
845 Third Avenue
New York, NY 10022
Tel: 212-759-5227
Fax 212-754-9320
or toll free 800-753-9696
Date ordered _____
❐ Received

Netherlands Board of Tourism
355 Lexington Ave., 21st Floor
New York, NY 10017
Tel: 312-819-0300
Fax: 212-370-9507
Date ordered _____
❐ Received

Northern Ireland
(See British Tourist Authority)

Norwegian Tourist Board
(see Scandinavia)

Poland
Orbis, Polish Travel Bureau
342 Madison Avenue, Suite 1512
New York, NY 10173
Tel: 212-867-5011
or toll free 800-788-7247
Fax 212-682-4715
Date ordered _____
❐ Received

Portuguese National Tourist Office
590 Fifth Avenue, 4th Floor
New York, NY 10036
Tel: 212-354-4403
Fax: 212-764-6137
Date ordered _____
❐ Received

Romania National Tourist Office
573 Third Avenue
New York, NY 10016
Tel: 212-697-6971
Date ordered _____
❐ Received

Russian National Tourist Office
800 Third Avenue, Suite 3101
New York, NY 10022
Tel: 212-758-1162
Fax: 212-758-0933
Date ordered _____
❐ Received

Scandinavian Tourist Board
(Denmark, Finland, Iceland, Norway, and Sweden)
655 Third Avenue, 18th Floor
New York, NY 10017
Tel: 212-949-2333
Fax: 212-983-5260
Date ordered _____
❐ Received

Scotland *(see British Tourist Authority.)*

Tourist Office of Spain
665 Fifth Avenue
New York, NY 10022
Tel: 212-759-8822
Fax 212-980-1053
Date ordered _____
❐ Received

Swedish Tourist Boar
(See Scandinavia)

Swiss National Tourist Office
608 Fifth Avenue
New York, NY 10020
Tel: 212-757-5944
Fax 212-262-6116
Date ordered _____
❐ Received

Turkish Tourism & Info. Bureau
821 United Nations Plaza
New York, NY 10017
Tel: 212-687-2194
Fax: 212-599-7568
Date ordered _____
❐ Received

Wales *(See British Tourist Authority)*

Yugoslavia (formerly)
Call U.S. State Department
for advisories (202-647-5225)

Notes

Notes

Step 3—Determine how much $$$ you will need

"Take half as much luggage," the saying goes, "and twice as much money." Good advice. For the purpose of this discussion, however, we're going to assume you can't take twice as much money. In fact, our guess is you're wondering where to get any extra money at all; lack of money is the first reason most people give for not traveling. We know, however, that you can travel, and on much less than you may think possible.

How? First, by valuing travel itself, and by acknowledging its importance to you. You can do this by knowing that it is not the first-class hotels and five-star restaurants you will remember, but rather the people you meet, the places you see, and the experiences you have; and by caring about those experiences, places, and people enough to sacrifice some (but not all) comfort, and to risk confronting the unexpected.

Second, by making your highest priority saving money for your trip. Would you rather go to Europe or buy a new stereo? A coat you don't need, or the Côte d'Azur? Go to Italy or go to a movie? (Every little bit counts.) Travel to England or remodel the kitchen? Take this trip or buy a new car? (Or how about selling your car and putting the money into a trip fund, as we did? We rode bikes for six months, lost weight, gained health, and had a great trip.)

A young man we know, planning a year-long trip to Asia and Africa, gave up drinking everything but water. He saved what he would have spent on soft drinks, coffee, and alcohol, and put the money toward his trip. This kind of saving may not net large sums, but it provides a powerful symbol to you and others that your goal is important and achievable.

Finally, you can afford to travel if you plan carefully, and that begins with knowing exactly how much to save. Here's a method for determining what you will need.

1. Estimate what you can comfortably live on each day. This figure includes all expenses in Europe that you haven't prepaid: food, sightseeing, entrance fees, souvenirs, gifts, lodging, and occasional transportation—cabs, buses, a single train trip, and ferries. (See below for a more complete list.)

Expenses *not* included in the daily budget are transportation to and from Europe, *prepaid* Eurail passes or long-term car rental, and the expense of maintaining your home or apartment while you are away.

Unfortunately, there is no magic formula to help you with this figure, which is highly personal and arbitrary. To get an idea of current costs, peruse guidebooks like *Fodor's, Frommer's, Lonely Planet,* or the *Let's Go* series, which include prices and descriptions of hotels, restaurants, fees for museums, etc.; talk to people who have recently traveled in the same area, and study the prices advertised in newspapers and magazines. Then decide what your own comfort level demands and go from there. When planning your budget, keep in mind that being on the move costs more than staying put. Travel days, whether you're driving, flying, or going by rail, will always require more money.

2. Multiply the daily expense figure you've settled on by the number of days of your planned trip. (Add at least two extra days' expenses to cover the first few days after arrival, when costs always exceed estimates.) Having a daily budget guarantees that you won't end up with a two-day supply of money and a two-week supply of time. Some people set aside their daily limit and spend only that amount; others skimp for a few days, then splurge on theater tickets or a great restaurant. Whatever you prefer, a daily budget is essential for planning purposes and saves money and frustration in the long run.

3. Now add all major expenses, like prepaid airfare, car rental, or Eurail passes.

4. The total of items two and three, above, will closely approximate your total trip cost. Can you afford it? If it's too much, take a look at your daily expenses—can they be reduced? Are less expensive hotels possible? Are you willing to take a room without a bath? How about hostels? Would a smaller car work as well? Can you divide your time between camping and hotels? Have you thought about limiting your travel to a smaller area? Perhaps renting an apartment?

There are myriad ways you can reduce expenses without jeopardizing your fun or your safety, and we've listed some of them below. When you start your own research, you'll find more. Some of them will require more effort on your part, but it will be effort well spent.

Once your budget is determined, post it in a convenient place. We have always used a small blackboard, which is perfect for this purpose because it is easily updated. (An example is shown on the following page.) If you have doubts about your trip really happening, nothing works better than seeing the "income" column add up, even in small increments.

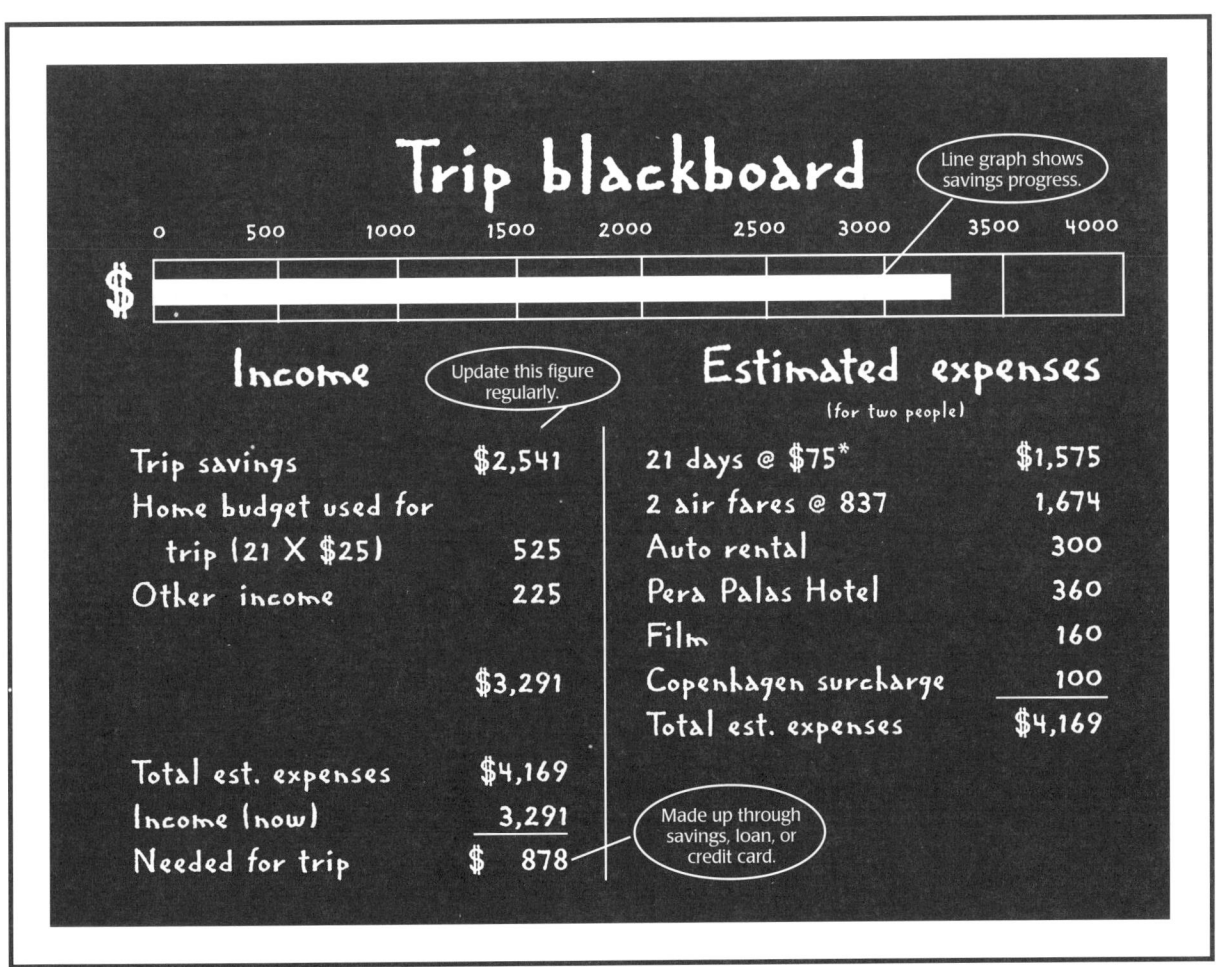

Recreation of authors' blackboard 30 days before a three-week trip to Turkey in 1993.
*On this trip we splurged. For instance, three of us traveled for six months in 1977 on $25 per day; in 1987 we traveled six months on $40 per day.

Expenses to plan for

- Pre-trip expenses. These include the cost of a passport or renewal, travel insurance, visas, extra photos, and "necessary" gadgets like converters and plugs or a dual-voltage hairdryer. By starting your planning early you can stretch these expenditures over a longer period of time.

- Getting to and from the airport. All major European airports are served by trains, buses (public, airline, hotel), and taxis, and a good travel agent can tell you the price of each method of transportation into town. Or consult *From the Airport to the City* (Houghton Mifflin, 1992), available in many libraries and bookstores. It will tell you what public and private transportation is available, how much it costs, how long it takes to get into town, and more.

- Lodging on arrival. Even if you plan on hitching, camping, or hosteling in Europe, make hotel reservations for the first and perhaps second night after arrival. It takes time to get over jet lag and to get your bearings. (Imagine arriving late in the day, in a strange city, after several plane changes. You've been awake for 36 hours, you're exhausted and irritable, and you have no place to stay. You are severely tempted by the first familiar place you see—an expensive American chain hotel. You may sleep well, but your budget takes a beating before you're even under way.)

- Gasoline if you're driving; plus a few dollars a day for in-city transportation—light rail, buses, and taxis—for the times you don't want to drive. (Train travelers will also need to add in-city transportation costs.)

- Ferry crossings. If you're traveling with a car, crossings are expensive. In 1994, for example, the crossing from Dover, England to Calais, France was $108–115 for a car and two people (ferry); and $84–$285 (hovercraft) depending on number of passengers. Chunnel crossings—the new passenger train service from London to Paris through the English Channel tunnel—are priced at this writing from $152 to $312 depending on class of service (based on $1.60 to the British pound).

  The ferry crossing from Italy to Greece for two people and a car is about $450, and this often increases in mid-July. (Advance ferry reservations are a must if you are traveling with a car over popular routes in the summer months. Plan to check in at least two hours in advance.)

- Camping gear, if purchased abroad (available in department stores and specialty shops in every major European city).

Tip: *Spend your money down before crossing borders to avoid paying a second commission on it when you change to a new currency. Note that banks and other exchange places only handle bills or major coins, such as the British pound coin.*

- Sightseeing expenses—Eiffel Tower, boat rides in Amsterdam, museums, bus tours, castles, and more. Current costs for major sights can be found in most guidebooks.

- Food. You do have to eat, and eating in Europe is one of the great pleasures of traveling there. But you don't have to eat in expensive restaurants to sample the local fare—it's all around you, everything from street vendors and working-class bistros and pubs to five-star dining rooms. Sample prices can be found in the same guidebooks that provide housing costs.

- Souvenirs and gifts for the folks who stayed at home. ("I never take gifts home," says a friend of ours who lived for many years in Europe. "I tell them, if they want something from Europe, come and get it.")

- If your trip is a lengthy one, include the cost of replenishing supplies like shampoo, deodorant, and shaving necessities.

- Build in a cushion for emergencies, changes in plans, unexpected events, or sites you didn't know about but can't bear to pass by.

Money-saving suggestions

- Shop around for your airline ticket. Call every airline that flies to your destination city, and call several travel agents as well. Check the ads in the travel section of your newspaper. The Council for International Education Exchange (CIEE) has about 400 offices around the country and is a good source for inexpensive flights. CIEE also offers a broad range of information about low-cost travel, and educational and work opportunities abroad. Write to them at 205 E. 42nd Street, New York, NY, or call 212-661-1412. To locate the office nearest you, call 800-438-2643.

- Be flexible. We once saved several hundred dollars by moving our departure date to take advantage of an inaugural fare. Those don't come around often, but money can be saved if you are willing to look for flights leaving at inconvenient hours or days. The same strategy works for train travel; early morning and night trips are often cheaper.

- Courier flights are worth considering if you can travel *very* light, leave in an instant, and have flexible return plans. See Kelly Monaghan's *The Insider's Guide to Air Courier Bargains: How to Travel World-Wide for Next to Nothing* (Intrepid Traveler, 1994, 3rd ed).

- Picnic. Europeans love to picnic, and there are lots of places to purchase good bread, cheese, meats, and prepared foods. This is much less expensive than eating in restaurants, just as much fun, and it's still local cuisine.

- Eat your big meal at noon, instead of the more expensive dinner hour.

- Shop around for restaurants—all post menus outside. Avoid heavily touristed areas where prices are always higher. Take a bus or underground train to an outlying part of the city—you will find restaurants less expensive and often more interesting.

- Remember that it's almost always more expensive to eat outside than inside, and in cafés it's less expensive to stand up than to sit.

- University areas are good places to find inexpensive restaurants and hotels. Some universities rent dormitory rooms during the summer months. National and local tourist offices can provide information about this service.

- Eat what Europeans eat, and be willing to experiment. Order the house specialities whenever possible, and you will generally get the best regional food and the lowest prices.

- Your breakfast is probably included in the price of your room, and other meals may be too—be sure to ask, and then take advantage of it. Typical breakfasts are bread and butter and jam with coffee; sometimes including cheese, meat, olives, or tomatoes. Unless you are really homesick, don't order traditional American-style breakfasts—you will pay dearly.

- Street vendors offer a variety of inexpensive foods, and we often partake of their wares. Caution is probably warranted, but we've never become ill as a result of this.

- Avoid cities and you will save money without even trying.

- A hotel room without a bath is less expensive than one with, and the inconvenience is minor. It is often assumed by hotel employees that

Americans want rooms with baths, so be sure to specify. If you're scrimping, ask for the hotel's smaller, less conveniently placed rooms.

- If driving, avoid motorway (freeway) restaurants and other concessions, which are very expensive. Know how many liters your gas tank holds (one U.S. gallon equals 3-3/4 liters; in Britain an imperial gallon equals 1.2 U.S. gallons) and whenever possible, purchase oil and other automotive supplies before you get on the motorway.

- Car rentals are always less expensive if rented ahead of time, in the U.S. However, if you are already in Europe, must have a car, and can wait 48 hours before you pick it up, you may save as much as half the cost by having a friend in the U.S. make the reservation for you.

- Day or weekly passes for city transportation are a better buy than individual trip tickets.

- Most major museums have a weekly free day (but you will have to deal with crowds).

- In Britain, consider purchasing a National Trust membership or a Ticket to View for the many stately homes, castles, etc. (See the Royal Oak Foundation in Resources). Check with national tourist offices for similar passes in other countries.

- If you are traveling on a Eurail pass consider taking night trains to save the cost of a hotel. A friend reports he "went weeks without accommodations, spending alternate days on opposite sides of Europe," and making good use of his pass. Be sure to protect your baggage while you sleep.

- If you like to read, take books with you. English language books are expensive and often hard to find. When you've finished with those, look for other English readers with whom to trade. Hostels are a good place for this.

- Senior and student discounts are often available. If you're eligible, watch and ask for them.

- Many credit cards now offer airline mileage credit, and a free flight will certainly reduce your trip budget. It's not necessary to go into debt to take advantage of this benefit; buying necessities and paying the balance off each month earns just as many miles.

Tip: Don't be caught short by unexpected holidays. Check the calendars sent by national tourist offices and those given in guidebooks, and make sure you have enough money to see you through a bank holiday.

Foreign currency

Tip: Check with your bank before departure: you may need a special PIN (personal identification number) in order to use your credit card in an ATM abroad.

Many travel books recommend taking a small amount of foreign currency with you, so that on arrival you'll have money for tips, telephones, taxis, and other small expenditures. We agree with this in principle, though we usually take off without it and have never been stuck.

It's not hard to find a place to change money on arrival, and if you haven't brought foreign currency with you, your first step will be to find an exchange office or ATM machine. Major airports and rail stations have banks or other changing facilities, which are usually open 24 hours a day. You usually pay more in commissions, or receive a less-than-generous exchange rate in these places, but sometimes convenience is all.

We have met Americans traveling in all-inclusive tours who never exchange money, spending only American currency during their entire trip. We cringed when a busload of Americans descended on a Swiss shop and one of them loudly asked a companion, "Do they take real money here?"

It is unfortunately true that if you stay on the tourist route, you *can* spend American dollars in shops, hotels, and some restaurants. We think this is a bad idea. It's arrogant; it's insulating; and the exchange rate is guaranteed to be awful. This is not the kind of trip you want to take.

Changing money might be easier if you think of it as "just like shopping"—you are buying and selling a commodity that happens to be cash, and it's a very simple transaction: you present your traveler's check or cash, and your passport, at the teller window; state the kind of currency you wish to purchase (lira, kroner, francs, marks) and the teller figures the exchange rate and pays out the money—usually minus a commission.

It's an excellent idea to carry a pocket calculator with you and calculate the amount of money you are to receive before you complete the transaction, then count your change before leaving the window. We're not suggesting that banks or others will deliberately cheat you, but transactions are swiftly handled, and mistakes can be made. Careful travelers do well to keep an eye on their cash. (The gadget-oriented can find calculators specifically programed for exchange transactions.)

Where and how you change money can make a difference to your budget over a period of weeks or months, especially if the budget is a small one. Besides airports, railroad stations, and banks, border crossings, some large department stores, some information offices, and most hotels and shops that cater to tourists will have money-changing facilities. In deciding where to cash your traveler's checks, note the exchange rate plus the service charge (commission), if any. You may get a better exchange rate at one location, but have to pay a high service charge, which cancels your gain. The more often you change money, the more often you pay a service charge, so plan ahead and limit exchanges. American Express and Thomas Cook will not apply a service charge when cashing their own traveler's checks, but their rates are not always the best. The point is, shop around. It's *your* money.

Remember that European banks—especially in small towns—may keep irregular hours, closing early one day a week, or closing for an unexpected holiday. Always make sure you have enough cash to see you through a weekend.

If you do want to purchase money before you go abroad, don't wait until the last minute, even if you live in a metropolitan area. The bank may have to order currency, and this can take several days. The fees charged for purchase of foreign currency are generally higher in this country than abroad.

Credit cards or traveler's checks?

The increasing availability of ATM machines makes it tempting to forego traveler's checks and depend only on ATMs for your cash needs. ATMs usually issue currency at bank wholesale rates, plus a small percentage charge, so the rate is often better than when cashing traveler's checks. But relying *only* on machines isn't a good idea. What happens if you can't find an ATM machine (quite possible), or if your card is "eaten," lost, or damaged?

We recommend that you also carry travelers checks, preferably drawn on a major bank or credit card. American Express, Visa, Mastercard, and Thomas Cook are most common and easiest to change. Traveler's checks can be purchased at banks, credit unions, and American Express offices. You will have to pay a one- to two-percent fee for the checks. Telephone those institutions and check on rates before you buy. We are able to buy AmEx checks for a better rate from our credit union than from the local American Express office. The American Automobile Association offers American Express traveler's checks free to AAA members.

If you're traveling to more that one country, it's usually best to purchase traveler's checks in U.S. denominations. If you will be in only one country, you may want to consider buying traveler's checks in that country's currency. Your decision must be based on where you will be, for how long, and whether the U.S. dollar is rising or falling in relation to other currencies. These can be very "iffy" considerations, and the decision can only be your best estimate.

Traveler's checks in foreign currencies may be cashed more easily (especially in out-of-the-way places) and may save you the change fee charged by banks and others. However, if the dollar is rising on the international currency exchanges, you will increase your travel fund by carrying travelers checks in U.S. denominations. Of course, the opposite is also true.

Finally, using credit cards—for cash or charging—is as convenient in Europe as it is in this country. Visa, American Express, Diner's Club International, and MasterCard are all accepted in Europe. All these companies offer similar services, including collision damage waivers, medical and legal referral assistance, emergency ticket replacement, emergency message service, lists of ATM locations, airline mileage accumulation, and more. Most American Express offices abroad also provide mail service (including mail forwarding), personal check cashing, and English-speaking staff. Call or write to your card issuer a few months before you leave and ask for a brochure detailing their travel assistance programs.

When using a credit card, check the amount shown on the receipt for misplaced decimal points, commas, and digits. This is the time to correct errors, if any. Then keep all receipts until you receive the final bill. If a dispute arises, and you don't have the original receipt, you will probably have to pay the incorrect amount.

Value added tax (VAT)

The value added tax (VAT) is a kind of national sales tax applied in 19 European countries. The amount varies from 6.5 percent in Switzerland to 25 percent in Denmark. It applies to car rentals, accommodations, restaurant meals, and purchased goods. It is possible to recoup the tax paid on purchases in shops, under certain conditions, but the process can be time-consuming and involves confusing red tape. Many stores also require a minimum purchase, which can vary widely. However, if you make major purchases in a single store, applying for the tax refund could be worth your time and energy.

There are many variations to this procedure, but *in general* it works like this. You get a tax-refund form from the merchant and fill it out when you make your purchase. If the store subscribes to the international refund service, Europe Tax-free Shopping, you will be given a certificate in lieu of the refund form.

When you leave the European Union you must have your refund form or certificate stamped by a customs official (you may be asked to show the merchandise). Certificates can then be redeemed at a VAT refund desk or designated bank in airports or train stations (usually less a 20 percent handling fee). At major airports you can now redeem certificates from any country, and receive payment in any currency. Refund forms, however, must be mailed after you return home and you will have to wait for your refund.

Note: If you *rent* a car while in Europe you will be charged a VAT. However, if you *lease* a car from the U.S. (usually a 21-day minimum), value added taxes do not apply. This can mean considerable savings.

Step 3 / to do...

1 Following the plan outlined in this chapter, complete the "basic budget" below, using the information currently available to you. Put these figures in a convenient place where you will see them every day and can easily make changes.

Basic Budget

$_____ = your estimate of daily expenses

x number of days: _____ = $ _____

\+ airfare: $ _____

\+ car rental/rail pass: $ _____

= total trip expenses: $ _____

---

2 Start saving! Economists suggest that we fritter away ten to twenty percent of our monthly income, and that we could save that much painlessly. Using today's date, calculate how much you need to save per week (or month) to meet your trip budget goals. (Be sure to include savings already accrued.) Write that figure here: $_____

3 Write or call the institution that issues the credit cards you will be taking on your trip. Ask them to send information about the travel services they provide.

4 Get out your calculator and, using the chart on page 37, calculate how many French francs you would receive in exchange for (a) $20, (b) $50, (c) $60, and (d) $100, in both traveler's checks and currency. Congratulations! You're now an international banker. (For answers see page 38.)

Taking the mystery out of money exchange charts

The exchange rate chart shown below is typical of those seen across Europe. This particular rate chart was seen outside a Paris bank a few years ago. Note that there is only one price for traveler's checks, compared to separate buy and sell rates for currency.

"Rate of Exchange Fees & taxes already deducted"

COURS NET DES DEVISES
FRAIS ET TAXES DEDUITS

Traveler's checks

Rate for American money

Currency

		Billets		Travellers
		Achat (bank buys)	Vente (bank sells)	SC
USA	1 US	5 45 FF	5 71 FF	5 54 FF
CANADA	1 CAN	4 57	4 80	4 59
RFA	1 DM	2 32	2 44	2 34
AUTRICHE	100 SH	0 33	0 346	0 332
BELGIQUE	100 FB	0 1395	0 1465	0143
DANMARK	100 KRO	0 735	0 78	0 74
GRANDE BRETAGNE	1£	11 20	11 80	11 27
ITALIE	1000 LR	4 65	5 05	4 72
NORVEGE	100 KRO	0 95	1 00	0 95
SUEDE	100 KRS	1 09	1 145	1 11
SUISSE	1 FR	2 62	2 75	2 649
ESPAGNE	100 PTA	0 058	0 062	0 059
PORTUGAL	100 ESC	0 087	0 097	0 088
FINLANDE	100 FIM	1 22	1 30	1 26
JAPON	100 Y	0 0240	0 0253	0 0247

The top line on the chart shows the rates for exchanging one U.S. dollar. For example, you have a $50 bill (billet) and want to change it into French francs (FF). The French bank is going to buy it (achat) and give you 5.45 FF for each dollar. Multiply your $50 by 5.45 and you can see that you will receive 272.50 FF. Generally you will receive a better rate if you exchange traveler's checks. In this example, for $50 in traveler's checks, you would receive 277 FF or about one dollar (1.7%) more. This can add up over the course of your trip. *Note:* Some charts have buy and sell columns for traveler's checks as well.

Notes

Answers to money-changing exercise: *Traveler's checks:* (a) 110.80, (b) 277, (c) 332.40, (d) 554. *Currency:* (a) 109, (b) 272.50, (c) 327, (d) 545.

Step 4—Improve your foreign language skills

Trying anything new means dealing with anxiety, and travel, despite the fact that it's usually thought of as relaxing, can generate a lot of anxieties. Chief among these is concern about not speaking the language—a reasonable fear that can be understandably inhibiting.

"What happens if I get sick?" you may think. "What happens if I get lost?"

We shamefacedly admit that, like most Americans, we are language poor. Between the two of us we speak some Spanish and a bit of Russian, and a continuing study of languages—or talk of study—is always with us. Though we do manage the basics, proficiency eludes us, and our failure is forcefully brought home on every trip abroad.

Nevertheless, we still travel, and our lack of a language has never created an insurmountable problem. It has often been frustrating, frequently time-consuming, and occasionally humorous, but it's never been a disaster. Help is (almost) always at hand. For instance:

- Highway and street signs are easily understood icons:

- Airports and train stations display signs in several languages, and use icons such as these:

- Tourist bureaus and information offices—marked by the ubiquitous —usually have English-speaking attendants.

It might be reassuring to know that English has become the second language of choice around the world, and it's common to hear travelers from different parts of Europe—for instance, a Swede and a Greek, or a German and a Spaniard—communicating in English. This doesn't excuse Americans for not knowing French or Spanish or German or Greek, but it does make travel easier. On each trip we've made over the years, we've found more and more English spoken everywhere. When it wasn't spoken, we became adept at sign and body language, learned to draw pictures of what we needed (always carry a pen and small notebook), used a phrase book or dictionary, or asked help from a student. (Some people like the new electronic translators, which work well when short phrases or words are needed. We prefer personal communication, however flawed it may be.)

Children in many countries study English in school, and they're usually delighted to practice by giving directions or other help. We've also learned to look for travelers from the Netherlands, because nearly all the Dutch speak English. ("Our nation is founded on trade," a woman from the Netherlands told us, "and it's imperative that we speak many languages well. It's required of all children in our schools.") Once a young Dutchman, who had never seen us before, even acted as a translator during a visit to a French-speaking doctor.

By all means, if there's time, study the language(s) of your choice. If that's impossible, purchase a phrase book or language tapes—Berlitz has a complete series of both—and *learn the courtesy words* (hello, goodbye, yes, no, please, thank you, etc.), *safety words* (help, police, fire, I'm lost, etc.), and *numbers* in the language of every country you plan to visit. You *can* manage that, and it will enhance your visit and your understanding. Everyone will appreciate your effort—even the French—and no one will laugh at you. And if they do, so what?

Do as much as you can manage, then don't let *not* speaking a foreign language prevent you from traveling. You may miss, or misunderstand, cultural complexities and nuances, for without the language one can never truly understand another culture. But you can still get around, enjoy, and learn from what you're seeing. Your patience may be stretched thin at times, but if you can relax and laugh at your own mistakes, you'll find it's worth it. And much easier than you think.

(And there are some advantages. You may find relief and relaxation in not knowing, since news broadcasts, newspapers, and television cease to be compelling when the words cease to be understandable. We once traveled six months with only one *International Herald Tribune* and one *Newsweek* to break the blissful peace.)

Step 4 / to do...

1. Check the library or a bookstore for language tapes and use commuting time to listen. If they're available, rent movies in that language. Consider hiring a tutor to help, or trade language lessons for a skill you possess. If near a college or university, you may be able to find a student/tutor who's a native speaker.

2. Call a nearby community college and ask if they teach conversational French, German, Italian, Spanish, Russian, or whatever. Sign up.

3. If you already know a foreign language, dig out old textbooks and brush up, *or* do one of the above.

4. If there's no time for any of the above, purchase a phrase book and learn the courtesy words and numbers. This is easy, essential, and will be much appreciated. An English-whatever pocket dictionary comes in very handy as well.

Notes

Step 5—Choose your transportation

Air travel

Not only is air travel generally uncomfortable and irritatingly impersonal, it's frustrating trying to find the right flight at the right fare. And there are no simple rules. If you know a good travel agent, start there. He or she will need your departure and return dates, departure city, stopovers, if any, and destination. Ask the agent to research current fares and get back to you. Even if you're comfortable with the results, you may discover a lower fare if you check with other agents and call airlines directly. Don't be surprised if every person you talk to supplies a different price; with deregulation, fares have become wildly erratic and can change suddenly. Be sure you understand all the restrictions that apply to a ticket before you purchase it.

Make your reservation as early as possible, but remember that reservations are only that: a space is being held for you. A fare quoted to you at the time may not be "locked in" until your ticket has been purchased, and fares can go up or down many times over a period of months. A travel agent can monitor seats and prices to provide you with the best possible savings, but many are unwilling or simply haven't the time to do this, and ultimately the responsibility is yours.

Tickets can also be purchased directly from airlines, or even from on-line computer reservation systems such as those offered by Compuserve, America Online, or the electronic Official Airline Guide (OAG). A list of airline telephone numbers is provided in the appendix.

It's sometimes true that the cheapest flight isn't always the best choice. For instance, a flight to London might cost much less than a non-stop flight to Paris. But if London is not your destination you will still have to pay to fly or ride the train to Paris. A stopover—even if you've always wanted to see London—may not be worth it. There may be a service charge attached to your layover, and a night or two in a London hotel could put a major dent in your budget. Weigh your options carefully: what looked like a bargain may turn out to be an expensive delay.

Tip: Using airline coupons purchased from a broker is risky, though tempting, and we reluctantly advise against the practice. Airlines will sometimes confiscate such tickets.

Rail travel

There is a school of thought—or unthought—which dictates that Americans who want to travel independently in Europe will do best if they purchase Eurail passes. This idea has become so ingrained that many travelers never consider other options. We think that's a mistake.

It is true that train travel in Europe does have advantages. Trains run frequently and on time, they are usually clean, and they go almost everywhere. Trains such as France's high-speed TVG, Italy's Pendolino, and Spain's AVE will whisk you between major cities at up to 186 miles per hour in comfort, and in some cases, elegance.

A Eurail pass is a good buy if you will be using it over long distances, if you will be traveling primarily in northern countries where train travel is more expensive, if you are traveling alone, or if you are absolutely panicked about driving a car in Europe. But other, limited passes are often a better buy, and a car rental/lease, when two or more adults are traveling together, is nearly always less expensive than purchasing two Eurail passes.

For example, a 21-day adult first-class **Eurail pass** in 1995 cost $648. A **Flexipass**, allowing 15 days of travel in two months, is $740 (and you lose the versatility of the standard Eurail pass); a **Saverpass** for 15 days (only for two or three people traveling together), is $430. Those under 26 can save by purchasing a **Youth Flexipass** (second class) allowing 10 days of travel in two months for $398. A **Europass**, is good for shorter trips within five countries: Spain, France, Germany, Italy, and Switzerland. The pass is priced from $280 to $660 and is for between five and 15 days of travel in three to five countries.

By comparison, a small 4-passenger automobile can be leased in Paris for 27 days for $632 (1995 price), including VAT but not collision damage waiver insurance (CDW). Gasoline, of course, is extra, and must be a consideration.

If you want to travel by train, and will be traveling in only one country, consider purchasing a pass from that country's state-owned railroad. France,

Germany, Spain, Scandinavia, and others offer rail passes similar to Eurail but limited to a country or area and therefore less expensive. For example, travel for four days out of 15 days in France is $179 first class, or $119 second class. Britrail offers five days' travel in 15 days for $335 first class, $249 second class, and $199 youth. A German rail Flexipass is $130 (adult, second class) for five days in one month, $200 for 10 days. Junior passes are $90 and $120, respectively.

If you're only planning one or two long train trips, ask about other passes and money-saving fares. For instance, the French National Railways offer free family passes (spouse and children travel half fare), youth passes for those under 26, and others. Some of these passes carry minor restrictions as to travel dates, and some of them cost an additional small fee. Nearly every European country offers rail passes similar to these.

Sometimes you can save money by simply taking the train at an earlier or later hour. Don't be afraid to ask for money-saving fares. You can find out about them at the train station, of course, and from local travel agents (for instance, American Express offices, where English is usually spoken), and from national and local government-sponsored tourist offices. Many budget travelers prefer to take overnight trains, thus saving the cost of a hotel room.

Eurail also offers Rail 'N Drive programs that combine rail passes and rental cars. These arrangements can be confusing, so request detailed brochures and study them well. Misunderstanding the restrictions and requirements could have a devastating affect on your plans.

Tip: When traveling on British Rail, including the London underground and bus service, keep your ticket with you until you disembark, when you may be asked to show it. When traveling on French trains, remember to date-stamp your ticket as you enter the platform. Tickets are not considered valid unless date-stamped.

A summary of rail passes in Europe and Britain

What follows is a summary of most available rail passes. Passes must be purchased in the United States and may be obtained from travel agents, from Rail Europe, Inc., and from specialty travel dealers. A pass may be purchased well in advance, since it does not go into effect until the first time it is used.

Prices, restrictions, and conditions of rail passes are all subject to change. Make sure that you read the fine print and understand all the conditions and restrictions.

EURAIL PASS—Good for unlimited and unrestricted rail travel on any or all days for the duration of the pass in 17 countries. Good in Austria, Belgium, Denmark, Finland, France, Germany, Greece, Holland, Hungary, Republic of Ireland, Italy, Luxembourg, Norway, Portugal, Spain, Sweden, and Switzerland. The pass in not valid on privately owned railroads in Spain and Switzerland.

EURAIL SAVER PASS—Saver passes require that two or more people travel together between October 1 and March 31; or three or more people must travel together between April 1 and September 30. Passes are available for 15 days, 21 days, and one month.

EURAIL FLEXIPASS—First-class travel limited to five days of travel in two months, ten days of travel in two months, or 15 days in two months.

EURAIL YOUTHPASS—Unlimited second-class travel for anyone under 26 years of age. Passes available for 15 days, one month, or two months.

EURAIL YOUTH FLEXIPASS—Limited second-class travel for anyone under 26 years of age. These passes are good for any five days of travel in two months, any ten days of travel in two months, or any 15 days of travel in two months.

BALTIC RAIL CARD—good for unlimited train travel throughout the three Baltic republics. Passes are available for eight and 15 days; for information call Eurocruises, 212-691-2099 or 800-688-3876; Uniontours, 212-683-9500 or 800-451-9511.

BRITRAIL PASS—Unlimited first-class or standard rail travel in England, Scotland, and Wales for the duration of the pass. Passes are available for periods of eight days, 15 days, 22 days, and one month. Senior (60+) and youth passes are also available.

BRITRAIL FLEXIPASS—Good for rail travel any four days in eight, eight days in 15, or 15 days in one month. Youth passes only are also available for 15 days travel in two months. Senior (60+) passes also available.

BRITRAIL also offers combination passes: BritFrance, BritGerman, BritIreland, England/Wales, special London services, and others.

FRANCE RAIL PASS—Unlimited first- or second-class rail travel, free transfer from Orly or Roissy Airports to Paris and back, discounts on Bateaux Parisiens cruises on the Seine, and more. Passes are good for any three rail travel days in one month. Additional rail days (six maximum) are also available. Children 4–11 years travel half-fare; children under four travel free.

Also available for purchase in the United States are France Rail 'N Drive passes and France Rail 'N Fly passes.

French railroads also offer family and youth cards that offer discounts for travel on certain days. Information is available in France at railroad stations and information offices.

GERMAN RAIL FLEXIPASS—One-month passes can be purchased with a varying number of travel days: five, ten, or 15. Reduced rates if you are under 26, and for two adults traveling together; children 4–11 pay half the adult fare, children under four travel free.

SWISS FLEXIPASS—Swiss Pass and Flexipass offer unlimited travel on the entire network of the Swiss Federal Railways, including lake steamers, postal motorcoaches, and most private railroads. Also available are one-month/one-round trip Swiss Card and Swiss Rail 'n Drive passes. Passes of varying length and travel days are available. Children under 16 travel free with a parent.

SPAIN FLEXIPASS—Passes are available for three days of travel in one month, eight days in one month, or ten days in one month. Also available is a Spain Rail 'N Drive package. Children 4–11 travel half fare; under four travel free.

HUNGARIAN FLEXIPASS—Five travel days in 15, or ten travel days in one month. Children 4–12 pay half the adult fare, children under four travel free.

CZECH FLEXIPASS—Unlimited first-class rail travel throughout the Czech Republic. Any five travel days in 15; children 4–13 pay half fare, under four travel free.

POLRAILPASS—Unlimited first- or second-class rail travel throughout Poland. Passes are for eight days, 15 days, 21 days, or one month. Discounts for those under 26 years of age. Children under ten travel at half fare.

EUROPEAN EAST PASS—Good for travel in Austria, Czech Republic, Hungary, Poland, and Slovakia. Five days of travel in 15, or 10 days of travel in one month. Children 4–11 travel half fare, those under four travel free.

SCANRAIL PASS—Passes are for four days in 15, nine days in 21, or 14 days in one month. Children 4–12 pay half the adult fare; those under age four travel free. Good for travel in Denmark, Norway, Sweden, and Finland; includes free and reduced rate ferry services linking Denmark, Sweden, and Finland.

Car rental, lease, or purchase

Several years ago a TV commercial portrayed a young French woman visiting America for the first time. "Americans drive so neat," she said. And compared to Europeans, it's true. Americans do drive "neat." We obey traffic signals and speed limits, stay within the white lines, use turn signals, and generally follow the rules.

Europeans, on the other hand, ignore traffic lanes, park haphazardly—often on sidewalks—don't signal, and usually drive faster than we are used to. An American accustomed to the relatively sedate and orderly freeways and turnpikes of this country can quickly turn to jelly when faced with a high-speed Italian autostrada, a London roundabout, or German autobahn (where you *must* stay out of the fast lane unless you are passing.)

Tip: If your plans include ferry passages with an automobile, keep in mind that rates are charged according to the length and/or weight of the automobile. Smaller cars will be less expensive to rent, fuel, and ferry.

However, driving outside major European cities and away from high-speed motorways is very much like driving here at home. And if you want the luxury of going where and when you want, stopping when you feel like it, eating when you are hungry, and visiting only what interests you, then by all means consider renting, leasing, or even purchasing a car. If you are planning to camp—a great way to see Europe—the flexibility of a car or camper van will add greatly to your convenience and comfort.

We think traveling by automobile is by far the most interesting way to see Europe. We've managed to drive over 25,000 miles in Europe with only one, very minor accident, and we've seen and enjoyed places and people we would never have found traveling any other way. We have leased cars, rented cars, and purchased cars—both new and used. In every case the arrangements were simple and easily handled.

It is always less expensive to rent or lease your car *before* leaving the United States. If you will be renting for a period of three weeks or more, a *lease* arrangement known as purchase/repurchase will eliminate the value added tax (VAT), which can range as high as 25 percent. Some travelers find a purchase/repurchase plan saves money even if they use the car for a shorter period of time.

Renault, Peugeot, Europe by Car, Foremost Euro-Car, Kemwel, and other companies offer these arrangements. For a price that is much lower than renting, you will get a new car with unlimited mileage and all insurance paid. Under the purchase/repurchase plan you are considered the owner of a personal car, and may have the responsibility for upkeep if enough miles are logged. For instance, we had to spend a day in Cannes while our Renault underwent a scheduled servicing—not a great sacrifice.

Whether you rent or lease, rates will vary from country to country. If your plans are flexible enough you will save money if you think ahead and ask about these varying rates. Auto Europe, for example, advertised 1994 weekly rates ranging from $527 (Germany) to $857 (Italy) for the same four-door sedan (tax and CDW included).

If you're up to a challenge and have the extra time, it's possible to buy a used car in Europe at one of the many used car dealers. Check classified ads in the *International Herald Tribune* and other newspapers, or buy a car from a traveler who is on the way home. Popular places to pick up used cars from other travelers are the Belevedere Road market near Hungerford Bridge, and in front of Australia House, both in London; and in front of the American Express offices in Amsterdam and Paris. The advantage is that these travelers probably speak English (many are Australians and New Zealanders who like to spend large blocks of time traveling) and have been through the process of registering and insuring a car. If you buy in Britain, however, you may have to deal with right-hand drive.

There is also an auto flea market on weekends in Paris near the Malesherbes Metro station.

When buying a used car, expect to pay cash and plan to insure and register the vehicle promptly. A registration fee will be charged, and, except in Britain, value added tax. A statement from your own insurance company that you are accident-free, or a copy of your state driving record, may get you lower insurance rates. Insurance companies are plentiful throughout Europe.

Bringing a used car home is possible, but there are many restrictions due to smog-emission control devices and safety standards. Permission from at least three government agencies is required. The best place to start is the U.S. Customs Service Public Affairs Office, 1301 Constitution Avenue N.W., Washington, DC 20229; Tel. 202-927-1770.

If a new European car is in your budget, buying it abroad can save money, especially if you keep it out of the U.S. for at least three months after purchase. This means you will be importing it as a used car and will pay lower duty. We once purchased a new VW camper bus that we drove for six months, shipped home, and sold for about what we paid for it in Europe, effectively giving us a trip free of in-Europe transportation and housing costs. Check with your local dealer, or ask the rental agencies listed below for information. Many of them can arrange a new-car purchase.

The primary drawback to driving is the high cost of gas in Europe. Gasoline is heavily taxed, and prices range from $2.50 to $4 per gallon. (European cars generally get better mileage than U.S. cars—a few up to 60 mpg.) Toll

Tip: Oil-company credit cards are not accepted in European gas stations. Mastercard or Visa may be accepted in some stations along major expressways.

roads, too, can eat more than spare change, and if you're on a tight budget it's best to avoid them. Germany's autobahns are free, but you will pay to drive the high-speed motorways of France and Italy.

Traveling the two-lane roads of Europe, however, is pleasant and free. Road surfaces are generally good, and you will see more sights and meet more people than you ever would on a four-lane expressway. And that's why you travel, isn't it?

When planning your route, estimate driving distances and time very conservatively. European countries appear so small compared to the U.S. that our inclination is always to try to see too much too quickly. European roads, though good, are often slow. Many of them trace ancient footpaths leading from settlement to settlement, and they still take you into the center of every village and town, greatly slowing your progress. Build in extra time for discovering unexpected sights and meeting unexpected people, for they are what make your travels memorable. We recommend not averaging more than 100 miles a day, and in some places even that is too much. You can decide to drive a little each day and keep moving at a relaxed pace; or you can stop and savor places more fully, then drive longer distances every three or four days.

Driving requirements

Most rental agencies require drivers to be at least 18 years old; some require you to be 21. You must show a valid U.S. driver's license, and in some countries an International Driving Permit as well. Even if not required, we recommend carrying a permit, because it is official-looking and understood everywhere. Permits are easily obtained from your local AAA office for $10 and two 2"x2" passport-style photos. Insurance will be provided by the rental agency and, depending on the country, you may be given a "green card" as proof of insurance, along with your rental papers. It's unlikely, but possible, that you will be asked to show your green card when crossing borders. Never leave these papers in the glove compartment of your car; *always carry them with you.*

Tip: Check the expiration date on your driver's license before you leave home, and renew if necessary.

If you have a less-than-perfect driving record, ask the rental company if they run checks on driver's licenses. Some travelers report getting to their destination, only to find their car reservation refused because of a poor driving record.

International Driving Permit

Shown below is a sample application form used to obtain an International Driving Permit from the American Automobile Association. This form can be obtained from any AAA office.

APPLICATION for INTERNATIONAL DRIVING PERMIT or INTER-AMERICAN DRIVING PERMIT

FEE FOR EACH PERMIT $10.00

Issuance of Permit is restricted to persons EIGHTEEN YEARS or over who hold a valid U.S.A. or Territorial License. PERMIT VALID FOR ONE YEAR. Not renewable.

CHECK DESIRED PERMIT

☐ International Driving Permit
(Fee $10.00 and 2 Passport Type Photos signed on back)

☐ Inter-American Driving Permit *** (see reverse side)
(Fee $10.00 and 2 Passport Type Photos signed on back)

MANDATORY REQUIREMENTS

(1) Attach 2 recent signed Passport Type Photos (2" x 2")   (2) Enclose permit fee of $10.00 (NO CASH)

NOTE: IT IS IMPORTANT THAT YOUR U.S.A. OR TERRITORIAL LICENSE BE CARRIED WITH THE PERMIT AT ALL TIMES. The International or Inter-American Permit is not valid for driving in the United States.

Mr. Mrs. Ms. (Circle One)   PRINT NAME IN FULL. No Initials

FIRST	MIDDLE	LAST
PHONE	HOME STREET ADDRESS	
CITY	STATE	ZIP CODE
U.S. DRIVER'S LICENSE NO.	STATE OF ISSUE	EXPIRATION DATE
BIRTHPLACE: CITY	STATE OR COUNTRY	BIRTH DATE (MO. DAY YEAR)
DATE PERMIT TO BE EFFECTIVE	DEPARTURE DATE FROM U.S.	
FOREIGN ADDRESS (If known)		

SAMPLE

PLEASE CHECK THE APPROPRIATE BOX BELOW TO INDICATE THE TYPE OF VEHICLE FOR WHICH YOU NOW HOLD A VALID U.S.A. OR TERRITORIAL DRIVER'S LICENSE, AND FOR WHICH YOU DESIRE THIS PERMIT:
☐ MOTORCYCLE ☐ PASSENGER CAR ☐ VEHICLE OVER 7,700 LBS. ☐ VEHICLE OVER 8 SEATS ☐ VEHICLE WITH HEAVY TRAILER

I CERTIFY THAT THE ABOVE INFORMATION IS TRUE AND CORRECT, AND THAT THE LICENSE INDICATED HAS NOT BEEN SUSPENDED NOR REVOKED.

I FURTHER CERTIFY THAT I UNDERSTAND THAT A VALID STATE DRIVER'S LICENSE MUST ACCOMPANY THIS PERMIT, AND THAT THIS PERMIT IS VALID ONLY AS LONG AS THE STATE LICENSE IS VALID, BUT NOT TO EXCEED ONE YEAR FROM THE DATE THE PERMIT IS ISSUED.

SIGNATURE (signature mandatory for issuance of Permit)	DATE

Courtesy of the American Automobile Association.

Collision damage waiver (CDW)

Collision damage insurance covers the insurance deductible when you are at fault in a motor vehicle accident. When you rent an automobile, you are usually asked to pay a premium, from $10–$20 daily. If you decline the CDW insurance offered by the renting agency they may place a "hold" of several thousand dollars on your card. This means that credit will not be available to you until the car is returned.

If you charge the cost of your rental on certain credit cards—Visa Gold, Amex, etc.—the collision damage insurance requirement may be waived by the renting agency. This waiver will mean big savings for you. However, in late 1993, credit card companies began limiting CDWs. If you are planning to charge your car rental on a credit card, we urge you to clarify all insurance coverage (and know how to file a claim) with your credit card company, and with the company from which you plan to rent. Lease (purchase/repurchase) plans generally include collision damage waivers, but it is up to you to read the fine print in any contract you sign.

The situation in Italy is even more confusing, since because of high losses due to auto theft in that country, rental companies are requiring renters to buy—in addition to CDWs—separate theft-protection policies, ranging (in 1995) from $10–$20 a day. This additional theft charge may be covered by your credit card.

Be sure you inquire about and understand all fees that may be charged on any car rental. These can include airport surcharges, drop-off fees, theft protection, VAT or other taxes, CDW, and personal accident insurance. (This is another good reason for renting from the U.S. before you leave home. Your contract will be in English.)

Tip: Visitors driving in Italy with foreign license plates (or who rent cars from the Rome or Milan airports and can show plane tickets) can receive free roadside assistance from the Automobile Club of Italy by dialling 116. English-speaking operators will send a tow truck to take your car to the nearest garage. The cost of repairs, or any further towing, will be the owner's (or renter's). This service is due to expire Dec. 31, 1995.

Auto lease / rental / purchase

Auto Europe Tel. 800-223-5555
27 Pearl Street
Portland, ME 04112
Rentals, leasing, and purchase. Wide selection of models.

Auto France, Inc. Tel. 800-572-9655
139 Sherwood Drive
Ramsey, NJ 07448
Offers a purchase/repurchase plan for Peugeot models, similar to that offered by Renault. Michelin maps and *Red* and *Green Guides* are also offered for sale.

Avis Rent-a-Car   Tel. 800-331-2112
Models vary by country. One-ways available.

Europe by Car   Tel. 800-223-1516
One Rockefeller Plaza
New York, NY 10020
Tax-free leases and rentals. Many models, including campers. Claims lowest prices for students and teachers. Offers economy hotel rooms for as low as $23 per night. One-ways available.

Foremost Euro-Car   Tel. 800-253-3876
5658 Sepulveda Blvd., Suite 201
Van Nuys, CA 91411
Rentals, leases. Models vary depending on country of lease. Campers and motorhomes also available. One-ways available.

Hertz Rent-a-Car   Tel. 800-654-3131
Models vary by country. One-ways available.

Kemwel Group   Tel. 800-678-0678
106 Calvert Street
Harrison, NY 10528
Advance reservations get lower rates. Rentals, leases, and purchases of most European models; campers available.

Renault European Delivery Services   Tel. 800-221-1052
650 First Avenue
New York, NY 10016
Lease (purchase/repurchase) a new Renault, including unlimited mileage, taxes, and insurance. Many models available. Three-week minimum.

Boat and ferry travel

Europe is laced with navigable rivers and canals, and traversing the continent by boat is not only possible, it's done by many people every year. The drawback, of course, is that you must have the boat, the knowledge, and the experience to make such a trip.

If you lack all these, but still yearn to be on the water, you'll find plenty of opportunities in Europe. The QE2 still makes periodic Atlantic crossings, and a few cruise lines offer trips from

the Caribbean to Europe. There are canal boat and "hotel barge" tours on the English, Dutch, and French canals (most of which are very expensive), and in some places you can rent a boat to operate on your own. You can take day trips or extended river cruises on the Thames, the Seine, the Danube, the Rhine, and others. And you can travel easily on ferries between England and the Netherlands, Belgium, and France. In the Baltic ferries run between Denmark, Sweden, Norway, Finland, Estonia, and Russia. Ferries also ply the waters from Italy to Greece, and Greece to Turkey. Among the many islands that can be visited by ferryboat are the hundreds of Greek islands, the Italian islands of Sicily and Sardinia, France's Corsica, Spain's Baleares islands, and Britain's Channel Islands.

If seeing the sights from the deck of a boat appeals to you, ask the national tourist offices for information, or call your travel agent, or the companies listed below that provide river and/or canal cruises or boat rentals in Europe:

Abercrombie & Kent International, Tel. 800-323-7308 or 708-954-2944 in Illinois. Luxury canal and river cruises, walking and biking trips.

Cruise Company of Greenwich, Tel. 800-825-0826 or 203-622-0203 in Connecticut. Canal boats in France, Ireland, and England. Luxury Mediterranean cruises.

Cunard, Tel. 800-221-4770
Trans-Atlantic travel on the QE2 and European river cruises.

Europe Cruise Line, Tel. 800-688-3876 or 212-691-2099 in New York. Overnight cruises in the Baltic, Rhine, and Danube rivers, Mediterranean, and more.

European Waterways (agents for LeBoat), Tel. 800-922-0291 or 201-342-1838 in New Jersey. Many river and canal cruises, plus good selection of "drive yourself" boats.

French Country Waterways, Ltd., Tel. 800-222-1236 or 617-934-2454 in Massachusetts. Luxury canal-boat cruises in France.

Julia Hoyt Canal Cruises, Tel. 800-852-2625 or 508-535-5738 in Massachusetts. Luxury trips with American hosts.

K.D. River Cruises of Europe, Tel. 800-858-8587 or 415-392-8817 in California. River cruises on the Rhine, Danube, Elbe, Moselle, Main, Seine, Rhône, and Saône rivers.

Premier Selections, Tel. 800-234-4000. Tours and self-drive boats available.

OdessAmerica Cruise Company, Tel. 800-221-3254 or 516-747-8880 in New York. Cruises in the Baltic, Mediterranean, and trans-Atlantic.

Get a map!

We once took a five-week driving/camping trip through the western part of the Soviet Union, and before we left home we were repeatedly warned: "Take road maps—the Soviet ones aren't accurate. They don't let their own people have reliable maps."

We sought in vain for Russian maps and arrived in the USSR to exclaim in wonder at the unreliability of the road maps Intourist, the Soviet tourist agency, had given us. Even the elaborate Russian gazette we purchased in Leningrad was wrong. Rivers showed up on the wrong side of the road. Towns, with their crucial and infrequent gas stations, could be as much as 20 miles distant. A paucity of road signs and unreliable maps meant that we were often lost, and more than once we were directed (or escorted) back to the "correct" road by a scowling and heavily armed policeman.

Good maps are crucial to happy traveling. Purchase maps—especially city maps—ahead of time and study routes into and out of major cities. Few European cities are built in neatly plotted squares, and unlike cities in this country, where you can simply turn right four times to find yourself back in the same place, turn right four times in London, Amsterdam, Paris, Rome, or Madrid, and you're likely to find yourself two miles away and headed in the wrong direction. A good map will eliminate arguments and frustration, and save you time and gas. If space is limited (and it should be) and your choice is between carrying guidebooks and carrying maps, carry maps.

There are many good European maps available, among them maps published by Michelin, Revenstein, and Hallwag. You will save money by purchasing them in this country, and you'll have the added advantage of being able to study them before you go. Bookstores specializing in travel should have them, or be able to order them. If there is no source in your town, write to one of the specialty bookstores listed in Resources. Tourist offices may include free maps in their packets of information; some of these are excellent. Michelin sells detailed area maps of France that are smaller and more manageable than its full-size map of that country.

Tip: A compass is an invaluable aid, whether you're walking or driving. It's easy to lose your way in the twisting streets of a European city, especially at night, or when it's overcast and you can't get your bearings. A compass takes up almost no room, but along with a map, it can save you time, gas, and frustration. By all means take one, and know how to use it.

Step 5 / to do...

___ 1. Four to five months before your trip, request information about rail passes and/or car rentals. Reserve or order as soon as plans are definite.

___ 2. Make airline reservations as soon as travel dates are firm.

    ___ A. Confirm seat assignments with airline—*don't* assume your travel agent has done this. (See page 93 for seats to avoid.)

    ___ B. Confirm your reservation 48 hours before departure *and* before your return flight. (Many airlines have discontinued this requirement, but it can't hurt to do so.)

___ 3. Purchase maps for the major cities you will be visiting.

___ 4. Order International Driving Permit. Check to be sure your state driver's license doesn't expire while you're abroad.

___ 5. If traveling in high season, make ferry crossing reservations, if needed.

Rail passes ordered on _____
                                                 (date)

from _____
                    (company or individual)

Cost of pass $ _____ x nr. of people ____ = $ _____

Method of payment : _____

Automobile rental/lease ordered on _____
                                                          (date)

from _____ Car model _____

for _____ days (weeks) @ $ _____

Pick-up point: _____

Return to: _____

Method of payment: _____

Notes

Notes

Step 6—Choose your accommodations

After transportation, your biggest expense will be lodging. Most travelers assume they'll stay in hotels, but there are lots of other accommodation options—especially if you're willing to be a bit adventurous.

Hotels

Since you're in Europe to meet Europeans and to appreciate their lifestyles, we hope you'll avoid American chain hotels, which charge $150 per day and up, and where your fellow guests are likely to be other Americans. There are plenty of clean, well-run, and inexpensive hotels, pensions, auberges, zimmers, otels, bed-and-breakfasts, and guest houses. France seems to have more small, inexpensive hotels than any other country we've visited, but lodging is seldom difficult to find anywhere.

National tourist offices can provide lists and ratings of hotels by price, type of accommodation, amenities, etc. If hotels will be your primary accommodation, ask for these lists when you write for information. Other sources are the many money-saving travel guides, such as *Lonely Planet, Frommer's, Fodor's, Let's Go*, etc.; your travel agent (though travel agents often won't know about the inexpensive inn just out of town); and best of all, other travelers. We make a practice of asking others we meet during our travels about places they can recommend.

Booking a hotel in Europe is as easy as booking one at home. Don't be afraid to pick up the phone and call or fax a reservation. Most hotels—even small ones—will have someone on staff who speaks English, and if they're popular enough to be listed in guides, they are used to Americans asking questions. On our most recent trip we simply phoned the Copenhagen B & B we had selected from a guidebook, gave our arrival information to the English-speaking host, then faxed a confirmation. Simple, quick, easy.

Once in Europe, you can use the many room-finding services that are in every major airport and rail station. Inexpensive hotels are usually plentiful near railroad stations, and on the road you'll find small inns, hotels, and pensions. Don't wait until late in the day to find a room, however, especially during the busy season. Check in early. Even in outlying areas hotels fill early, and your day may end in a long and frustrating search—in the dark—for a nonexistent room.

If you're traveling on a budget, you can save money by asking for a room without a bath. We have seldom found this to be inconvenient, after an initial period of "getting used to." Hotel clerks often assume that Americans only want rooms with private baths, so be sure to specify if you don't.

It is also common practice in Europe to inspect the room before accepting it, and we urge you to do this. Don't be shy—in some places you'll be thought odd if you don't ask. If you don't like the room, simply say politely that you'd like to look further, and do so. In Greece and Turkey it's acceptable to haggle over the price of a room, but don't expect to make much headway during high season.

Tip: *Unless you're staying with friends or relatives, always make advance reservations for your first two nights in Europe—even if you plan to travel free of schedules and itineraries. You will undoubtedly suffer from jet lag, and you'll be in unfamiliar territory with a number of adjustments to make. Make it easy on yourself and stay put the first 24–48 hours.*

Youth hostels

Youth hostels, which are not limited to youths, are located nearly everywhere travelers want to go. A few are wonderfully situated in charming old castles, and a few others are simply awful. Most, however, are simple, clean, well-run establishments and are friendly stops for budget-oriented travelers of all ages. Hostelers are expected to bring their own linens (sheets—a sheet sleeping sack is most common—pillowcase, and towels), to share kitchen facilities, and to help clean up before departing. Facilities usually include dorm rooms segregated by sex, though many now have separate facilities for families or couples. A membership in American Youth Hostels is $10 for youths under 18, $25 for adults, $35 for a family, and $15 for seniors. Membership entitles you to special discounts on such things as museum fees, and rail, air, and ferry tickets. Write to American Youth Hostels, P.O. Box 37613, Washington, DC 20013-7613; Tel. 202-783-6161 for membership information and directories of hostels in Europe.

Apartments

Apartments are not usually considered an option by travelers, but we have found them to be a wonderful and inexpensive change from hotel life. This is especially true if you want a home base for your explorings, or simply want to know one area well. We've stayed in a tiny beach bungalow in Spain, a high-rise apartment in Portugal, an old stone farmhouse in central France, and a flat in Turkey with a wonderful view of the Aegean. All of these were found easily, usually within a day or two of our decision to stop awhile. Again, if you're traveling in high season in heavily touristed areas, you're better off making arrangements ahead of time. But we've always been lucky and found wonderful places on the spur of the moment.

One source for rentals is the local municipal tourist office. You can request these addresses from the national tourist office, or you can write directly to the Office of Tourism in the city or town where you wish to rent. It's best to allow at least 6–12 months for this kind of transaction, since vacation rentals usually book well ahead of time. Most rentals in resort areas are available for stays of a week or longer.

If your decision to rent is a spur-of-the-moment one, try not only the local tourist bureau, but real estate agents as well. Look around for a likely office, and simply go in and ask. With luck someone will speak a little English, and with perseverance you can make your wants known. Renting is easiest, of course, in resort/vacation areas like the Spanish coast, but don't lose heart if your ideal spot is an isolated mountain top. Ask around; chances are you'll find something you can live with. We found a charming house in central France by asking the owner of a café if she knew of any rentals. She closed the café and led us to a nearby real estate office that just happened to have a recent cancellation.

There are U.S. companies and real estate agents who specialize in rentals abroad, and their ads can be found in travel magazines and newspapers. If you're dealing with an unknown agency, it's a good idea to check with the local Better Business Bureau before paying out money in deposits or rent.

One caution—don't expect your European accommodations to be as efficient and trouble-free as your American home probably is. In Portugal we dealt with smelly drains, determined ants, an air conditioner that was "temporarily" away for repairs—leaving a gaping hole in the wall—and an elevator that stuck between floors. All this in a new, very modern, highrise.

In France, we lit a fire in the irresistibly quaint (and huge) fireplace and the "efficient" radiator attached to it erupted in an ear-splitting cacophony of clanging and screeching that drove us, temporarily terrified, into the night. An unfamiliar insect bred fruitfully in the light fixtures, and the living room furniture was "mixed lawn." Despite it all we were delighted to be where we were, and recommend such adventures.

Home exchanges

House exchanges are becoming increasingly popular, with many companies, "clubs," and agents offering this service. Their ads, too, can be found in travel magazines and in the travel sections of newspapers. We cannot make recommendations, as we have had only one unsuccessful brush with house exchanges, although we know people for whom it has worked well. We do suggest that you check with the local Better Business Bureau about the agency you choose, and that the references of possible exchange partners be checked.

Home exchange and rental organizations

Interhome USA, 124 Little Falls Road, Fairfield, NJ 07004; Tel. 201-882-6864, Fax 201-808-1742.

Intervac U.S., P.O. Box 590504, San Francisco, CA 94159; Tel. 415-435-3497 or 800-756-4663, Fax 415-435-7440.

The Invented City, 41 Sutter Street, Suite 1090, San Francisco, CA 94404; Tel. 415-673-6909 or 800-788-2489.

Loan-a-Home, 2 Park Lane, Apartment 6E, Mt. Vernon, NY 10552-3443; Tel. 914-664-7640.

Vacation Homes Unlimited, 18547 Soledad Canyon Road, Suite 223, Santa Clarita, CA 91351; Tel 805-298-0376 or 800-848-7927.

Vacation Exchange Club, P.O. Box 650, Key West, FL 33041; Tel. 800-638-3841, Fax 305-294-1448.

Homestays

A growing number of organizations will organize homestays with European families for you or your children. Homestays are a wonderful way to learn about a country's culture, language, and people, and most can be arranged for a very reasonable cost. They are best for people who can adapt easily, and who are willing to participate in household chores and in the daily life of another culture.

Elderhostel and World Learning—homestay programs for those 55 and older in 11 countries. Write to 75 Federal Street, Boston, MA 02110; or call 617-426-8056.

Federation of National Representation of the Experiment in International Living—one- to four-week homestays can be arranged through partner organizations in 17 countries. Write to P.O. Box 595, Main Street, Putney, VT 05346; or call 802-387-4210.

The Friendship Force—two-week homestays in 45 countries. Write to 57 Forsyth Street, NW, Suite 900, Atlanta, GA 30303, or call 404-522-9490.

Tip: *If you're planning to do your own laundry, remember that dark-colored towels and clothing dry more quickly in the sun than light colors.*

U.S. Servas—A $55 membership permits you to arrange an unlimited number of two-night stays with other members in 130 countries. Write to 11 John Street, Room 407, New York, NY 10038; or call 212-267-0252.

Camping

Have you considered camping in Europe? Do you know that many, many Europeans camp on their vacations, and that campgrounds are numerous—even in major cities? If your goal is to travel leisurely and cheaply and to meet Europeans, and if you're tolerant of minor inconveniences, we recommend camping. It's not the rustic, outdoor experience most Americans think of when the word "camping" is mentioned. Indeed, wilderness camping, so far as we know, does not exist in Europe. You will *usually* find:

- Shower and toilet facilities, and hot water—sometimes at extra cost. Facilities are sometimes clean, sometimes not.

- Grocery stores. These range from very small, bare-necessities stores to near-supermarkets in some resort campgrounds like the Lido campground near Venice. Campground stores, like convenience markets in this country, can be expensive.

- Restaurants. Some campgrounds have them, and if they do, they're worth a try. We've had very satisfying and inexpensive meals in campground restaurants.

- No delineated sites. Unlike most U.S. campgrounds, there are no clearly defined campsites with driveways, campfire pits, and picnic tables. Instead, the manager will point you toward an open field, and you can set up

wherever you choose. Because Europeans have a higher tolerance for crowding than Americans do, you may find yourself tent-peg to trailer-bumper with other campers, and out of necessity you'll find your patience and tolerance increasing as your trip continues—another of travel's free benefits.

- Elaborate tents, often more than one to a family group. Expect to find families bringing tables, chairs, TVs, stoves, refrigerators, and even the pet canary. Bicycles, inflatable boats, etc. are common.

- Some facilities may have automatic washers and dryers. We have seen them in campgrounds in Venice, Paris, and on the Spanish coast. In general, American-style laundromats are rare and expensive. If you're on a tight budget, plan to launder by hand.

- Be prepared for noise and dust, and look around for bright lights and loudspeakers before you set up your tent.

- Campgrounds can be found in city centers, small town parks, village greens and mountain tops; in fact, almost everywhere except the Spanish interior, where they are rare. You can even camp in major cities such as London, Rome, Paris, Amsterdam, and Madrid. In France you'll see signs advertising camping "a ferme," which means camping on someone's private land, usually with minimal facilities, but often peaceful and uncrowded.

- Campgrounds may be privately owned or operated by a camping or automobile club or a municipal or state body.

Some camping information can be obtained from national tourist offices. The Automobile Association of Britain publishes a camping guide for all of Europe. A good resource for France is the *Michelin Camping Guide.* If you plan to travel by train and camp, get *How to Camp Europe by Train* by Lenore Baken. Finally, *Europa Camping and Caravaning Guide*, a German publication, is highly recommended. It is updated annually and lists more than 4,000 sites, with maps, price lists, car ferry information, and camping discounts. This 600-page book may be too big to carry around, so consider tearing out or photocopying the pages you need. It is available at some bookstores, or by calling Recreational Equipment, Inc.; Tel. 800-426-4840.

It's possible to rent/lease a car and camping equipment, or you can take minimal equipment with you and purchase what you need. We once camped for three months, carrying only a lightweight tent and our sleeping bags on the flight over. In Paris we purchased a small camping-gaz stove, minimal cookware and table settings, and a folding table and chairs. After three months we returned to the Bois de Boulogne campground in Paris, set up a few "for sale" signs, and sold everything we had purchased to travelers just starting on their journey.

For longer trips, consider renting or purchasing a camping van. Camping vans, though expensive to buy or rent, are extremely popular in Europe and are available through a number of standard auto rental/lease agents. Used vans (the VW is especially popular with travelers) can sometimes be purchased from people who are finishing up long trips. See page 49 in the previous chapter for more information about purchasing used cars.

International Camping Carnet

This is a kind of camping passport which can be left at camping offices when you check in, in lieu of your passport. In some campgrounds the carnet automatically gives you a discount. You also receive "third-party liability insurance," which protects the holder and his or her party against personal or property damage to third parties incurred through camping activities. To obtain an International Camping Carnet in this country, you must join the Family Campers & RVers (formerly National Camper's and Hikers Association) for one year. Carnet applications can be obtained by calling 716-668-6242 or by writing to:

Family Campers & RVers
4804 Transit Road, Bldg. 2
Depew, NY 14043-4704

The cost is $30, and includes a mandatory one-year membership. Carnets are also available in some European campground administration offices, but it's easiest to get one before you leave home.

Courtesy of Family Campers & RVers.

Step 6 / to do...

__1__ Decide on a hotel in your destination city and make reservations for the first night or two after arrival. Call or fax them your reservation. A travel agent can also do this for you.

> Name of hotel: _____
>
> Address: _____
>
> Phone: _____
>
> Dates reserved: _____
>
> Price: _____
>
> How paid: _____
>
> Name of person taking reservation, if known:
>
> _____

Depending on your interests (or, if you're still undecided), do the following:

__2__ Write or call the American Youth Hostel Association, P.O. Box 37613, Washington, DC 20013-7613; Tel. 202-783-6161, and request information.

__3__ Write to Family Camping and RVers for information about camping in Europe and about camping carnets: 4804 Transit Road, Building 2, Depew, NY 14043-4704; Tel. 716-668-6242. Request camping information when writing to national tourist offices.

__4__ Interested in exchanging homes? Send a postcard to each of the agencies listed in this chapter and ask for information.

__5__ If the idea of homestays appeals to you, write for information. Addresses can be found on page 62.

Notes

Notes

Step 7—Order your passport

A passport is a document that identifies the holder as a citizen of the country that issued the passport. It contains identifying information about the holder (in this case, you), including date and place of birth, and a photograph. A passport is required for international travel. You may be asked to show it at border crossings, when checking into a hotel or campground, cashing a traveler's check, renting a car, or even using a credit card. Most important, it's your permission to enter the United States when you return home. Everyone, including newborn infants, is required to obtain a passport in their own name.

Passports are issued by the U.S. Department of State to U.S. citizens or nationals. There is a $65 fee for first-time applicants over 18, and the passport is good for ten years; applicants under 18 years pay a $40 fee for a five-year passport. Both fees include a $10 processing fee.

First-time applicants must complete and submit a passport application *in person* (unless the applicant is under 13 years of age) and provide (1) proof of U.S. citizenship, (2) proof of identity, (3) two identical photographs that meet requirements, (4) fees.

Any U.S. post office can provide information. Applications can be obtained at authorized post offices; at passport agencies in Boston, Chicago, Honolulu, Houston, Los Angeles, Miami, New Orleans, New York, Philadelphia, San Francisco, Seattle, Stamford, or Washington, D.C.; or they can be obtained by mail from Passport Services, Office of Correspondence, Department of State, 1425 K Street, NW, Washington, DC 20522-1075. If this is your first passport, request form DSP-11.

If you are renewing your passport, and if it has expired any time within the past 12 years, and if you were over 18 when it was issued, you may renew it by mail by completing the renewal form (DSP-82) and enclosing your old passport, two new photos, and a check or money order for $55.

Applying for or renewing a passport can take time—up to six weeks during the spring and summer—so don't wait until the last minute, unless you have no choice.

Finally, if you already have a passport, check to be sure it won't expire while you're abroad. For recorded information about passports, or to report one lost or stolen, call 202-647-0518.

Tip: Passport rush service, for an additional $30, is available to those who must travel within 10 days. Delivery of the passport is guaranteed within three days.

Visas

A visa is your permission to enter a particular country, and most visas limit the time you may spend there. Western European countries do not require tourist visas. Recent political changes in eastern Europe have caused visa requirements for those countries to be frequently revised. As of this writing, the formerly communist countries of Bulgaria, the Czech Republic, Estonia, Hungary, Poland, and Slovakia now permit visa-free entry for U.S. Citizens. Lithuania requires a visa ($25), as does Ukraine ($30) and Russia ($20–$60 depending on processing time. Russian visas require a sponsor, which can be an individual or organization). Romania also requires a visa. The fee is $30, and an itinerary and a letter stating the reason for your trip is required. Albania now permits group travel only, and visas are required. Turkey has recently reinstated visas for Americans. The fee is $20, and they can be obtained through any Turkish embassy or at the border.

In most cases visas may be obtained at border crossings, or at embassies or consulates, either in the U.S. or abroad. If you will be traversing a country on your way someplace else, you may wish to request a transit visa (usually good for three days). These are often less expensive than full tourist visas.

Passengers on trains passing through the Commonwealth of Independent States (the former Soviet Union) are required to have Russian visas, even if they are not stopping in CIS countries. For instance, if a train to St. Petersburg or Moscow makes stops in the Baltics or Ukraine, separate visas are required. Visas for the former Soviet republics are not available on trains; be sure you have what you need before climbing aboard. Transit visas are available but should be obtained before reaching the border. You may have to wait several days for processing.

For more specific visa information, call—well in advance—the embassy or consulate of the country you will be visiting and request the appropriate application forms. You will probably be asked to forward your passport to their office, along with the completed form and a small fee. Since most countries have embassies or consulates in Washington, DC, call DC information at 202-555-1212 and ask for the telephone number.

If you need a visa in a hurry, you can use a visa service, a private service that will, for a fee, obtain a visa for you, sometimes within 24 hours. Your travel agent can direct you to these services, or they may be found in the yellow pages in most large cities.

While it may be more convenient to get a visa while still in the United States, it is not required. Most countries have embassies or consular offices in the major European capitals, and spontaneous action is not out of the question. If you decide while in London that you want to visit Romania (or Turkey, Thailand, or Tanzania, for example), you may obtain a visa by going to the appropriate embassy in London, filling out the necessary forms, and paying your fee. A delay of several days is possible, but sometimes a whim is worth the wait.

Remember, visa regulations are subject to change; check *before* you get to the border.

Step 7 / to do...

If you already have a passport, check to make sure it won't expire while you're traveling. If renewing, or applying for a first passport, obtain the forms using the information on page 69 and follow the steps below. If you need more information, call 202-647-0518 (a 24-hour information line) or check with your local post office.

1. **For first-time passport applicants (who must appear in person):**
Complete the appropriate form(s) and attach, with each application:

   ___ a certified copy of your birth certificate*;

   ___ two identical photos (2x2 inches, color or black and white, taken within the last six months, full face, unretouched, front view in normal street attire), which are heat resistant. Vending machine photos, snapshots, and full-length photographs are unacceptable;

   ___ a check or money order for the correct amount.

   Date application(s) made:_____

   Date passport(s) received:_____

2. **For renewing applicants:**
Complete renewal form(s) DSP-82 and attach, with each application:

   ___ two identical photos (see above for details)

   ___ check or money order for $55 (mail applicants are not charged the $10 execution fee); and

   ___ your old passport (it will be returned). Mail to:

   > National Passport Center
   > P.O. Box 371971
   > Pittsburgh, PA 15250-7971

   Date application(s) mailed:_____

   Date passport(s) received:_____

___ 3 Purchase at least two extra passport photos to carry in case your passport is lost or stolen. (A photocopy of the first two pages of your passport will also help speed the process of replacement, should it be necessary.) Extra photos also come in handy for international driver's licenses (two), camping carnets (one), visas, and some rail passes. (Here's an example of when seven photos might be needed: two for a new passport, two for an international driving permit, one for a camping carnet, and two extras if your passport is lost.)

___ 4 Determine if you will ___ will not ___ need a visa on this trip. If yes, enter date(s) and countries for visa(s) ordered:

date requested	embassy/country
date requested	embassy/country
date requested	embassy/country
date requested	embassy/country

*In lieu of a birth certificate you may, if necessary, substitute a report of your birth abroad or your naturalized citizenship document. If none of these can be obtained, a driver's license, employee identification card, military ID, or student ID is acceptable. If none of these items are available, take a friend with you to the passport office or post office who has known you for at least two years and who has identification.

Notes

UNITED STATES DEPARTMENT OF STATE
APPLICATION FOR ☐ PASSPORT ☐ REGISTRATION
SEE INSTRUCTIONS—TYPE OR PRINT IN INK IN WHITE AREAS

SAMPLE

1. NAME — FIRST NAME / MIDDLE NAME / LAST NAME
2. MAILING ADDRESS — STREET / CITY, STATE, ZIP CODE / COUNTRY / IN CARE OF

☐ 5 Yr. ☐ 10 Yr. Issue Date _____
R D O DP
End. # _____ Exp. _____

3. SEX — Male / Female
4. PLACE OF BIRTH — City, State or Province, Country
5. DATE OF BIRTH — Mo. Day Year
6. SEE FEDERAL TAX LAW NOTICE ON REVERSE SIDE — SOCIAL SECURITY NUMBER
7. HEIGHT — Feet Inches
8. COLOR OF HAIR
9. COLOR OF EYES
10. (Area Code) HOME PHONE
11. (Area Code) BUSINESS PHONE
12. PERMANENT ADDRESS (Street, City, State, ZIP Code)
13. OCCUPATION
14. FATHER'S NAME / BIRTHPLACE / BIRTH DATE / U.S. CITIZEN ☐ YES ☐ NO
15. MOTHER'S MAIDEN NAME / BIRTHPLACE / BIRTH DATE / U.S. CITIZEN ☐ YES ☐ NO
16. TRAVEL PLANS *(Not Mandatory)* — COUNTRIES / DEPARTURE DATE / LENGTH OF STAY
17. HAVE YOU EVER BEEN ISSUED A U.S. PASSPORT? YES ☐ NO ☐   IF YES, SUBMIT PASSPORT IF AVAILABLE. ☐ Submitted
    IF UNABLE TO SUBMIT MOST RECENT PASSPORT, STATE ITS DISPOSITION: COMPLETE NEXT LINE
    NAME IN WHICH ISSUED / PASSPORT NUMBER / ISSUE DATE (Mo., Day, Yr.) / DISPOSITION

SUBMIT TWO RECENT IDENTICAL PHOTOS — 2" x 2" — FROM 1" TO 1-3/8"

18. HAVE YOU EVER BEEN MARRIED? ☐ YES ☐ NO   DATE OF MOST RECENT MARRIAGE — Mo. Day Year
    WIDOWED/DIVORCED? ☐ YES ☐ NO   IF YES, GIVE DATE — Mo. Day Year
    SPOUSE'S FULL BIRTH NAME / SPOUSE'S BIRTHPLACE

19. IN CASE OF EMERGENCY, NOTIFY *(Person Not Traveling With You)* *(Not Mandatory)*
    FULL NAME / RELATIONSHIP
    ADDRESS / (Area Code) PHONE NUMBER

20. TO BE COMPLETED BY AN APPLICANT WHO BECAME A CITIZEN THROUGH NATURALIZATION
    I IMMIGRATED TO THE U.S. (Month, Year) / I RESIDED CONTINUOUSLY IN THE U.S. From (Mo., Yr.) To (Mo., Yr.) / DATE NATURALIZED (Mo., Day, Yr.) / PLACE

21. DO NOT SIGN APPLICATION UNTIL REQUESTED TO DO SO BY PERSON ADMINISTERING OATH

I have not, since acquiring United States citizenship, performed any of the acts listed under "Acts or Conditions" on the reverse of this application form (unless explanatory statement is attached). I solemnly swear (or affirm) that the statements made on this application are true and the photograph attached is a true likeness of me.

Subscribed and sworn to (affirmed) before me — Month Day Year
(SEAL)   X _____
☐ Clerk of Court or
☐ PASSPORT Agent
☐ Postal Employee
☐ (Vice) Consul USA   At _____
(Signature of person authorized to accept application)
(Sign in presence of person authorized to accept application)

22. APPLICANT'S IDENTIFYING DOCUMENTS ☐ PASSPORT ☐ DRIVER'S LICENSE ☐ OTHER (Specify)
    ISSUE DATE — Month Day Year / EXPIRATION DATE — Month Day Year / PLACE OF ISSUE / No. / ISSUED IN THE NAME OF

23. FOR ISSUING OFFICE USE ONLY (Applicant's evidence of citizenship)
    ☐ Birth Cert.   SR   CR   City   Filed/Issued:
    ☐ Passport   Bearer's Name:
    ☐ Report of Birth
    ☐ Naturalization/Citizenship Cert.   No.:
    ☐ Other:
    ☐ Seen & Returned
    ☐ Attached

    APPLICATION APPROVAL
    Examiner Name
    Office, Date

24. FEE _____ EXEC. _____ POST _____

FORM DSP-11 (12-87)   (SEE INSTRUCTIONS ON REVERSE)   Form Approved OMB No. 1405-0004 (Exp. 8/1/89),

UNITED STATES DEPARTMENT OF STATE

PASSPORT APPLICATION

FEDERAL TAX LAW:

Section 6039E of the Internal Revenue Code of 1986 requires a passport applicant to provide his/her name (#1), mailing address (#2), date of birth (#5), and social security number (#6). If you have not been issued a social security number, enter zeroes in box #6. Passport Services will provide this information to the Internal Revenue Service routinely. Any applicant who fails to provide the required information is subject to a $500 penalty enforced by the IRS. All questions on this matter should be referred to the nearest IRS office.

ACTS OR CONDITIONS

(If any of the below-mentioned acts or conditions has been performed by or applies to the applicant, the portion which applies should be lined out, and a supplementary explanatory statement under oath (or affirmation) by the applicant should be attached and made a part of this application.)

I have not, since acquiring United States citizenship, been naturalized as a citizen of a foreign state; taken an oath or made an affirmation or other formal declaration of allegiance to a foreign state; entered or served in the armed forces of a foreign state; accepted or performed the duties of any office, post, or employment under the government of a foreign state or political subdivision thereof; made a formal renunciation of nationality either in the United States or before a diplomatic or consular officer of the United States in a foreign state; or been convicted by a court or court martial of competent jurisdiction of committing any act of treason against, or attempting by force to overthrow, or bearing arms against, the United States, or conspiring to overthrow, put down, or to destroy by force, the Government of the United States; or having been naturalized, within one year after such naturalization, returned to the country of my birth or any other foreign country to take up a permanent residence.

WARNING: False statements made knowingly and willfully in passport applications or in affidavits or other supporting documents submitted therewith are punishable by fine and/or imprisonment under provisions of 18 USC 1001 and/or 18 USC 1542. Alteration or mutilation of a passport issued pursuant to this application is punishable by fine and/or imprisonment under the provisions of 18 USC 1543. The use of a passport in violation of the restrictions contained therein or of the passport regulations is punishable by fine and/or imprisonment under 18 USC 1544. All statements and documents submitted are subject to verification.

PRIVACY ACT STATEMENT:

The information solicited on this form is authorized by, but not limited to, those statutes codified in Titles 8, 18, and 22, United States Code, and all predecessor statutes whether or not codified, and all regulations issued pursuant to Executive Order 11295 of August 5, 1966. The primary purpose for soliciting the information is to establish citizenship, identity, and entitlement to issuance of a United States Passport or related facility, and to properly administer and enforce the laws pertaining thereto.

The information is made available as a routine use on a need-to-know basis to personnel of the Department of State and other government agencies having statutory or other lawful authority to maintain such information in the performance of their official duties; pursuant to a court order; and, as set forth in Part 171, Title 22, Code of Federal Regulations (see *Federal Register,* Volume 42, pages 49791 through 49795).

Failure to provide the information requested on this form may result in the denial of a United States Passport, related document, or service to the individual seeking such passport, document, or service.

HOW TO APPLY FOR A U.S. PASSPORT. U.S. passports are issued only to U.S. citizens or nationals. Each person must obtain his or her own passport.

IF YOU ARE A FIRST-TIME APPLICANT, please complete and submit this application in person. (Applicants under 13 years of age usually need not appear in person unless requested. A parent or guardian may execute the application on the child's behalf.) Each application must be accompanied by (1) PROOF OF U.S. CITIZENSHIP, (2) PROOF OF IDENTITY, (3) TWO PHOTOGRAPHS, (4) FEES (as explained below) to one of the following acceptance agents: a clerk of any Federal or State court of record or a judge or clerk of any probate court accepting applications; a designated postal employee at a selected post office; or an agent at a Passport Agency in Boston, Chicago, Honolulu, Houston, Los Angeles, Miami, New Orleans, New York, Philadelphia, San Francisco, Seattle, Stamford, or Washington, D.C.; or a U.S. consular official.

IF YOU HAVE HAD A PREVIOUS PASSPORT, inquire about eligibility to use Form DSP-82 (mail-in application).

Address requests for passport amendment, extension of validity, or additional visa pages to a Passport Agency or a U.S. Consulate or Embassy abroad. Check visa requirements with consular officials of countries to be visited well in advance of your departure.

(1) PROOF OF U.S. CITIZENSHIP.

(a) APPLICANTS BORN IN THE UNITED STATES. Submit previous U.S. passport or **certified** birth certificate. A birth certificate must include your given name and surname, date and place of birth, date the birth record was filed, and seal or other certification of the official custodian of such records. A record filed more than 1 year after the birth is acceptable if it is supported by evidence described in the next paragraph.

IF NO BIRTH RECORD EXISTS, submit registrar's notice to that effect. Also submit an early baptismal or circumcision certificate, hospital birth record, early census, school, or family Bible records, newspaper or insurance files, or notarized affidavits of persons having knowledge of your birth (preferably with at least one record listed above). Evidence should include your given name and surname, date and place of birth, and seal or other certification of office (if customary) and signature of issuing official.

(b) APPLICANTS BORN OUTSIDE THE UNITED STATES. Submit previous U.S. passport or Certificate of Naturalization, or Certificate of Citizenship, or a Report of Birth Abroad, or evidence described below.

IF YOU CLAIM CITIZENSHIP THROUGH NATURALIZATION OF PARENT(S), submit the Certificate(s) of Naturalization of your parent(s), your foreign birth certificate, and proof of your admission to the United States for permanent residence.

IF YOU CLAIM CITIZENSHIP THROUGH BIRTH ABROAD TO U.S. CITIZEN PARENT(S), submit a Consular Report of Birth (Form FS-240) or Certification of Birth (Form DS-1350 or FS-545), or your foreign birth certificate, parents' marriage certificate, proof of citizenship of your parent(s), and affidavit of U.S. citizen parent(s) showing all periods and places of residence/physical presence in the United States and abroad before your birth.

(2) PROOF OF IDENTITY. If you are not personally known to the acceptance agent, you must establish your identity to the agent's satisfaction. You may submit items such as the following containing your signature AND physical description or photograph that is a good likeness of you: previous U.S. passport; Certificate of Naturalization or of Citizenship; driver's license (not temporary or learner's license); or government (Federal, State, municipal) identification card or pass. Temporary or altered documents are not acceptable.

IF YOU CANNOT PROVE YOUR IDENTITY as stated above, you must appear with an IDENTIFYING WITNESS who is a U.S. citizen or permanent resident alien who has known you for at least 2 years. Your witness must prove his or her identity and complete and sign an Affidavit of Identifying Witness (Form DSP-71) before the acceptance agent. You must also submit some identification of your own.

(3) TWO PHOTOGRAPHS. Submit two identical photographs of you alone, sufficiently recent to be a good likeness (normally taken within the last 6 months), 2 × 2 inches in size, with an image size from bottom of chin to top of head (including hair) of between 1 and 1-3/8 inches. Photographs must be clear, front view, full face, taken in normal street attire without a hat or dark glasses, and printed on thin paper with a plain light (white or off-white) background. They may be black and white or color. They must be capable of withstanding a mounting temperature of 225° Fahrenheit (107° Celsius). Photographs retouched so that your appearance is changed are unacceptable. Snapshots, most vending machine prints, and magazine or full-length photographs are unacceptable.

(4) FEES. Submit $65 if you are 18 years of age or older. The passport fee is $55. In addition, a fee of $10 is charged for the execution of the application. Your passport will be valid for 10 years from the date of issue except where limited by the Secretary of State to a shorter period. Submit $40 if you are under 18 years of age. The passport fee is $30 and the execution fee is $10. Your passport will be valid for 5 years from the date of issue, except where limited as above.

Pay the passport and execution fees in one of the following forms: checks—personal, certified, traveler's; bank draft or cashier's check; money order, U.S. Postal, international, currency exchange; or if abroad, the foreign currency equivalent, or a check drawn on a U.S. bank.

Make passport and execution fees payable to Passport Services (except if applying at a State court, pay execution fee as the State court requires) or the appropriate Embassy or Consulate, if abroad. No fee is charged to applicants with U.S. Government or military authorization for no-fee passports (except State courts may collect the execution fee). Pay special postage if applicable.

Step 8—Make your trip a safe one

Much as we like to think that traveling means escape from everyday cares and worries, we also have to admit that it means taking on new and unfamiliar ones. Is the water safe to drink? What if we get sick and can't find a doctor? Are the doctors well trained? What if I'm robbed? What about terrorists?

Everyone can relate tales of woe: lost passports, unexpected illness, stolen luggage—bad things do happen. But before going off the deep end, remember that most accidents occur in the home and that happiness has been shown to strengthen your immune system—two good reasons for hopping on a plane and flying off to exotic lands. In all our trips we've suffered only one serious case of diarrhea, the aforementioned fender-bender, and one car break-in with minor losses.

Thievery and other hassles

The most common risk is having your money, passports, and credit cards stolen. Thieves are everywhere tourists are, though not for the same reasons, and they are skilled in turning vacation into frustration.

For example, imagine the central police station in Rome. That staircase on your right leads to a small second-floor office, overflowing with unhappy travelers. They spill into an even smaller anteroom, where they perch impatiently on hard, straight-back chairs.

Near the only window sit a pair of dejected Australians who lost passports and traveler's checks when their car was broken into. Nearby is an American who discovered his wallet missing from his back pocket after he boarded a city bus. Next to him is an English woman carrying two straps—the remnants of an expensive handbag. On her left is another American whose car was ransacked. He lost a camera lens and credit cards. A Canadian found himself surrounded by children—and had his pockets picked.

Being burgled is upsetting, to say the least. Few can afford the loss of cash or the inconvenience of losing traveler's checks, credit cards—or worse—a passport. When you're in a city you don't know, confronted with a language you don't speak, such losses can leave you feeling bewildered and angry. They may also leave you wanting to put an end to a trip you'd planned for years.

Is there a way to avoid being part of this scenario? Not entirely, but the following steps can minimize your losses and make the experience a little less frustrating.

Protect yourself and your belongings

Begin with a simple but important step: count your luggage before you leave home, then count each piece every time you move it (include purses and camera bags in your count). Don't take your eyes off it in crowded airports and train stations. It's almost impossible not to let your attention be diverted occasionally, but those are the times experienced thieves are watching for. Get in the habit of resting your foot on a bag or its strap when you're standing, or wrap straps through a chair leg when you sit down. Keep your bags in front of you.

When going through airport security send a companion, if you have one, ahead to immediately collect baggage, purses, and camera bags as they come off the conveyor belt (yet another reason for not taking more than you can easily carry).

The most aggravating loss abroad is a passport. You need it to check into a hotel, to travel across a border, to cash a traveler's check, and of course you need it to get home. There is a simple device that will reduce the chance of this crucial loss, and that is a passport pouch. These are very common in Europe, and they're easy to find in U.S. shops that specialize in travel. They vary from a simple passport-sized pocket attached to a long drawstring, to a multipocketed, zippered, Velcroed, carryall. We recommend the simplest, lightest, flattest model you can find. Wear it around your neck and out of sight, under your clothes.

If there's room in the pouch, it's smart to slip in major credit cards and a few traveler's checks, too. *Always* carry passports on you, and if driving a car, your registration and insurance green card as well. *Never leave these documents in your car or luggage*—carry them, and you won't end up like the two Australians in the Rome police station.

Minimize your vulnerability

The two items most vulnerable to theft are purses and camera bags. Wear pants or skirts with deep pockets, and avoid purses altogether. (Once you get used to hands-free walking you may find it difficult to go back to a purse.) Fanny packs are convenient, but they're also easy to steal—a quick, sharp knife can cut through that strap before you know it. If you wear a fanny pack, attach the strap to your clothing with a heavy safety pin.

If you must carry a purse, make sure it's a shoulder bag. They're easier to hold onto and harder to grab away. Don't just prop it on your shoulder; wear the strap across your body, with the bag away from the street. Quick-acting thieves on motorbikes like nothing better than a dangling purse carried nonchalantly near a curb.

The same goes for a camera bag; avoid the expensive look, and carry it securely. A sturdy day-pack lined with foam will protect your camera and lenses and be easy to carry securely, and less obvious as a target. Many small cameras can be carried in pockets or attached to a belt.

If you're staying in a hotel, take the key with you if you can, rather than leaving it at the desk. Don't leave valuables loose in your room. When you leave, hang a "do not disturb" sign on the door. Many travel catalogs and shops now carry miniature alarms to hang on your door knob when you're in. If you're traveling alone, or worry about your safety, these are comforting to have along.

If you're renting/leasing a car, ask for one with a separate trunk and avoid hatchback models that expose your luggage to greedy eyes. Keep all valuables locked out of sight. Experienced thieves can break into most cars in a matter of seconds, so avoid displaying *anything* that marks you as a tourist. In some countries, rental cars bear special license plates which, unfortunately, alert thieves to your tourist status. If your car has such a plate, you'll need to be especially cautious about leaving valuables in the car (some travelers leave the empty glove box open to show thieves there's nothing of value there). Again, don't leave your car registration, rental papers, or insurance papers in the car. Carry them!

When traveling by train, keep hand luggage and other valuables between you and the window. If you must leave your bags in a vestibule, strap them to a handrail. If you intend to sleep, consider strapping the bags to your body in some way and stow your wallet or purse in an unreachable spot.

Never carry money or other valuables in obvious places. A wallet in a back pocket is an open invitation. Dress conservatively; try to blend in. Leave expensive jewelry at home in your safe deposit box—why spend your vacation worrying about such things?

Don't flash big wads of money. Try to figure out ahead of time how much your purchase will cost and what your change will be, and have the cash ready. Then count the change; don't let anyone rush you. If you can, avoid carrying bills of large denominations.

But what if it happens anyway?

What happens if, despite these precautions, you are robbed? Stoically prepare to deal with some red tape. You *must* file a police report in order to prove loss when applying for a new passport, or to replace stolen traveler's checks or other essentials (remember to keep a record of those checks). *Keep copies of all reports.*

Replacing lost items will be easier if you take the following steps:

- Photocopy everything you might need before you leave home, including credit cards, insurance cards, driver's license, receipts for traveler's checks, and your passport information pages. Photocopy both sides of your cards, or make sure you write down, on the photocopy, the phone numbers for reporting lost cards. You might want to make reduced-size copies and trim excess paper.

- Carry this copy separately from your passport and credit cards, and leave another copy at home with a friend. If your cards are lost or stolen, the person at home may be able to report the loss more quickly and easily. If you're traveling with a companion, you can each carry a copy of the other's information, and divide traveler's checks between you, too.

- If you have extra passport photos, carry them with the photocopied passport pages. If you need to replace a passport, the photos and photocopies will speed the process.

It's unfortunate that steps like this are necessary, but if you're prepared, even determined thieves needn't spoil your holiday. Safe traveling is a combination of common sense and good planning. Stay alert, and chances are your trip will be safe and worry-free.

A word to women traveling alone

Women are traveling the globe alone in increasing numbers, and many choose to start their journeys in Europe, where Western values and culture appear relatively familiar.

But despite this familiarity, Europeans *are* different (that's part of the fun of being there), and while you are trying to understand their motives and expectations, they may be making assumptions about yours. You should know that machismo still exists in Europe—particularly southern Europe—and that your independence and self-assertiveness may be misread.

Thanks to the thousands of Hollywood movies and television shows that have been exported abroad, the image of Americans in general and of American women in particular has been severely distorted, creating a mystique you may find hard to shake. There's not much you can do, single-handedly, to change this image, but there are steps you can take to increase your personal safety.

If you're planning to travel alone the *best* thing you can do is to take a self-defense class. You will learn useful and potentially lifesaving techniques, and as a bonus, you will find your self-confidence and self-esteem rising.

Once you're on your own, listen to your intuition—your "inner voice." If you feel something is wrong, change the situation immediately by moving away, getting on a bus, joining a crowd—whatever. Trusting your feelings and acting on them is your best defense.

Learn how to yell (practice!) and never be afraid to make a scene if you are threatened. Women mistakenly believe it is their responsibility to keep everyone happy, and every situation pleasant. Baloney. Better to be embarrassed than a victim. (A shriek alarm is worth considering too; they are small, inconspicuous, and loud.)

Avoid places where you might find yourself unexpectedly alone—beaches, out-of-the-way lanes, etc. Always be alert to your surroundings.

Emulate the European women around you. How are they dressed? Do they go alone into bars, tavernas, even restaurants? Are they walking alone, or with other women, or with men? When you are uncomfortable, or even uncertain, observe the locals and be guided by their actions.

If you do feel threatened, don't be shy about attaching yourself to strangers—other women, or a couple—until you again feel safe.

Finally, don't let worry steal your trip from you. Thousands of women travel by themselves every day. Take that self-defense class you've been promising yourself, find and read books about intrepid women travelers—there have been many and their numbers grow daily—and go and enjoy yourself.

Health care

Reasonably healthy people can travel in Europe with little fear of developing serious travel-related illnesses. If you are under a doctor's care, by all means talk with him or her before your trip.

If you regularly take prescription drugs, carry an extra copy of the prescription—preferably typewritten—stating the trade name, manufacturer, chemical name of the drug, and the dosage. Tuck it into your passport where it will be readily available if needed.

If you take digitalis, anticoagulants, or insulin, it is advisable to carry your own supply, but in general, the drugs available to you at home are also available in Europe.

A dental checkup is a good idea, especially if you will be traveling for some time, or have dental work which is causing problems. Emergency dental repair kits are available from specialty travel stores and catalogs.

We also recommend carrying an extra pair of eyeglasses, or a prescription, in case of loss or breakage. A stray dog once chewed up Ray's eyeglasses while he lay dozing in the shade of a 14th-century castle. The crunch of breaking glass woke him, but it was too late. Wisely, he had brought a back-up pair.

The most common problem for travelers is diarrhea, though Europe is considered by the U.S. Department of Health and Human Services to be a low-risk destination for that particular problem.

No one wants to be sick, however, and even though the risk is slight, there are steps you can take to minimize it.

- Drink bottled water, carbonated beverages, beer, wine, hot coffee or tea, or water that has been boiled or treated with iodine or chlorine. This is especially relevant if you are traveling in undeveloped parts of eastern Europe or the former Soviet Union, or if you are camping in out-of-the-way places.

- Avoid foods such as raw meat, raw seafood, and raw fruits and vegetables. Tap water, ice, and unpasteurized milk and dairy products are associated with incidents of illness.

That said, we must report that most travelers find it difficult to avoid these contaminants. Our policy has generally been to eat what we want and hope our bodies adjust to the new regimen quickly. In most cases, that has worked well.

Most traveler's diarrhea is self-limiting and requires only replacement of fluids and salts. Fruit juices, caffeine-free soft drinks, and salted crackers are good. Your doctor can give you a prescription for anti-diarrhea medicine, or you can purchase off-the-shelf remedies at home and in Europe (but you should know what you are buying). Some people believe yogurt and lactobacillus preparations are helpful preventatives.

If you do get diarrhea, the Center for Disease Control recommends drinking alternately from two glasses containing the following preparation: (1) eight ounces of orange, apple, or other fruit juice with 1/2 teaspoon of honey or corn syrup and a pinch of table salt added, along with (2) eight ounces of water with 1/4 teaspoon of baking soda.

If you develop chills or fever, or if the diarrhea is severe or does not cure itself within several days, then by all means seek out a doctor.

Finding medical help

A real concern for first-time and even repeat travelers is the fear of not being able to find an English-speaking doctor. There are several ways around this.

One good source is the International Association for Medical Assistance to Travellers (IAMAT) which guarantees members qualified medical assistance from an English-speaking physician, 24 hours a day. There is no cost to join, though donations are much appreciated. Members receive a booklet listing participating physicians around the world. These doctors agree to a set payment schedule for IAMAT members. In addition, the IAMAT offers climate charts and information on sanitary conditions for 1,440 major cities around the globe.

The IAMAT works to promote a standardization of medical care for travelers and operates as a non-profit organization supported solely with voluntary contributions. For more information, write to the membership office at 417 Center Street, Lewiston, NY, 14092 or call 716-754-4883.

Another source is your credit card company. Many card companies are offering services that include medical and other referrals. We have used the American Express Global Assist service with great success, and other cards offer similar help. Write or call them before you leave home and ask for a complete list of their services.

Finally, if you are near an American Embassy or Consular office, you can call for a referral. The embassy is under no obligation to provide referrals, however, nor will they pay for health care.

Several books on the market provide health information for travelers. One of the most complete is *Travelers Health: How to Stay Healthy All Over the World* by Richard Dawood, M.D. The U.S. government also offers health-related brochures. They are listed in Resources.

Travel insurance

One way to protect yourself and your belongings is to have travel insurance. If you purchase your airline ticket with a credit card, theft and baggage loss insurance may automatically be included. Before you purchase a separate policy, check with your credit card company.

Before purchasing insurance, especially medical insurance, ask how the insurance company pays a claim. Do they pay on the spot, or reimburse you after you get home? Pay-on-the-spot insurance is usually more expensive, but if the company does not pay "on-the-spot," *you* may have to, or risk having your passport held until payment is made.

Travel insurance may be purchased directly from insurance companies, from local insurance brokers, or from travel agents. Many companies specialize in travel insurance, and the variations and combinations are endless. The final decision must be based on your own personal requirements. Here are some of the options available:

Tip: *Your own insurance company may provide out-of-country coverage. If so, this will most likely be your least expensive option. Major credit cards are also a possible source of insurance. Check these possibilities before purchasing an additional policy, and be sure to carry a claim form with you.*

1) **Travel accident:** This coverage provides personal, around-the-clock protection against all accidental hazards. It usually includes injury due to accidents in all conveyances, such as plane, automobile, train, boat, bus and taxi. Coverage is determined by the amount of the principal sum selected.

2) **Optional sickness:** Coverage for sickness is usually an optional benefit, which is added to the accident coverage by paying an additional premium.

Your own health-insurance policy may cover you for accident or illness while you're abroad. Check with your insurance company to see what they cover and how they pay. Be sure to take a claim form with you.

3) **Trip cancellation**. This coverage provides protection for the non-refundable deposit or other fees paid by the insured (or covered family member) to participate in a trip that is prearranged by a travel agent. Purchasing trip cancellation insurance protects the amount of nonrefundable money you have paid for a trip, in case of death, accidental bodily injuries, or the illness of an immediate family member (even if they are not traveling with you). Default by a tour operator is also usually included, but if you're traveling with a tour company, be sure to verify this.

Trip cancellation insurance also protects you if you hold a non-refundable airline ticket and cancel your flight for a covered reason.

4) **Travel baggage.** Baggage insurance covers loss to personal effects accompanying you while traveling. There is usually a coverage limit on cameras, jewelry, watches, and precious gems. Most policies also pay a small amount to purchase necessities if your baggage is delayed for more than 24 hours.

5) **Emergency medical evacuation.** This covers cost of evacuation to the closest medical facility when the attending physician determines that adequate medical care is not available for you. It may also pay for your return home, if determined necessary by the attending physician.

6) **Flight insurance.** Flight insurance covers accidents that occur while boarding, riding in, or deplaning from your aircraft.

Insurance companies & medical referrals

Access America
P. O. Box 90315
Richmond, VA 23286

Tel. 800-284-8300
❏ requested _____
❏ received _____

Carefree Travel Insurance
100 Garden City Plaza
Garden City, NY 11530

Tel. 800-645-2424
❏ requested _____
❏ received _____

Health Care Global
Wallach & Co.
107 W. Federal St., Suite 13
Middleburg, VA 22117-0480

Tel. 800-237-6615
❏ requested _____
❏ received _____

Medex Assistance Corp.
1447 York Road, Suite 410
Lutherville, MD 21091

Tel. 800-537-2029
❏ requested _____
❏ received _____

Travel Assistance International
1133 15th Street, N.W., Suite 400
Washington, DC 20005

Tel. 800-821-2828
❏ requested _____
❏ received _____

Travel Insured International
P.O. Box 280568
East Hartford, CT 06128-0568

Tel. 800-243-3174
❏ requested _____
❏ received _____

Travel Guard International
1145 Clark Street
Steven Point, WI 54481-2980

Tel. 800-782-5151
❏ requested _____
❏ received _____

Tip: A pre-existing illness can void trip-cancellation insurance if treatment occurs within 60 days of the policy's effective date. Carry your policy with you and get documentation of all treatment.

Note: We urge you to obtain as much information as possible from these companies, and read the fine print. Know what you are buying!

Other helpful safe-travel information

Superintendent of Documents
U.S. Government Printing Office
Washington, DC 20402
> *Health Information for International Travelers*, $7
> *Camper's First Aid*, $2.50
> *Your Trip Abroad*
> *Travel Tips for Older Americans*
> *A Safe Trip Abroad*

Department of Transportation Travel Advisories
Call 800-221-0673 for recorded messages about current terrorist threats to U.S. citizens, and to air, rail, and other transportation systems at home or abroad.

Department of State Consular Affairs Bulletin Board
If you have a computer and modem, you can obtain information from the electronic bulletin board at 202-647-9225. Available through this service are such things as passport and visa information, emergency services abroad, consular information sheets about various countries, and travel information on specific subjects or regions.

For recorded U.S. State Department advisories and consular information, telephone 202-647-5225. Information can also be obtained through an automated fax service at 202-647-3000.

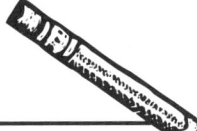

Step 8 / to do...

___ 1 Make several photocopies of the following items; leave one copy at home with a friend and carry the others separate from the originals. If you have a travel companion, you can carry copies of each other's documents.

- ❒ first two pages of passport
- ❒ all credit cards you plan to carry
- ❒ insurance cards
- ❒ driver's license

___ 2 Purchase a passport pouch to carry important papers and cards.

___ 3 Review current insurance coverage and determine if you will need additional coverage while traveling. If so, request information from the companies listed in this chapter.

___ 4 If taking medication, obtain copies of all prescriptions from your physician.

___ 5 If you wear prescription glasses or contact lenses, take an extra pair or carry a copy of your prescription.

___ 6 Join IAMAT (don't forget donation).

___ 7 If interested, order the U.S. government brochures listed on page 86.

___ 8 Review safety procedures before you depart. Remember to count your luggage pieces each time you move them. Be sure to include purses and camera bags in count.

Notes

Step 9—Start packing

There are two important questions to keep in mind when packing for a trip. The first is: how much will the airlines allow you to take? Ignoring this question may cost you money and cause you trouble.

The second is: how much can you carry? Ignoring this question may bring you pain and misery, and your answer will be with you throughout your trip.

Honestly, you can get by on far, far less than you think you can. Everyone can comfortably travel with only one small bag, no matter how long you plan to be away. Remember that you're going to be on the move; you will seldom see the same people twice—except your companions, who will be in the same boat—and everything you take will probably have to be carried by you. The best way to face this issue is to test-pack your bag(s), pick it up and carry it for several blocks (a quarter-mile would be more realistic) and see how you feel. Then go back and repack.

Small bags and backpacks have additional advantages. They can be carried on board by you instead of being misplaced by airline personnel. They fit easily through or over subway gates, onto train seats and overhead racks, and into the (probably) tiny trunk space of your rented car. They also fit in the small luggage lockers found in airports and train stations all over Europe. Large lockers are available but they are fewer in number and are often filled. Attended storage rooms can be found in some large train stations and airports. Expect to pay a small fee for this service. (To find lockers, look for the icon showing a suitcase and a key.)

If small bags or backpacks just aren't you, consider luggage carts or suitcases with wheels. If two or more people are traveling together, a good luggage cart can be loaded with several bags, and can save muscles and nerves on those long pulls through lengthy airport concourses, cavernous train stations, and seemingly unending hotel searches through city and village streets.

A luggage cart makes it easy to keep everything in one place, and it's certainly easier to get around. You will be tempted by this ease, however, to take more than you should. Resist this with all your might, for you will be surprised at how quickly that little cart gets overloaded: first your bag, then your companion's bag, then a camera bag, then a purse, then a shopping bag, then . . .

If you're purchasing a luggage cart, don't cut corners by buying a cheap one. We actually melted the wheels off an inexpensive cart, pulling it loaded over three kilometers of cobbles. Other cautions: small wheels don't work well on cobbled streets, and unprotected suitcase wheels may be knocked off when cases are handled in "normal" ways (airlines recommend removing them, though it's highly unlikely anyone does this). Put an I.D. tag on your luggage cart and carry it with you onto the plane. Don't strap it to your checked suitcase, where it may be damaged or lost.

If you are buying a new suitcase, we recommend the new roll-aboard type with retractable handles and wheels that are partially recessed, and therefore protected. Backpack/suitcase combinations are also good choices due to their compact design and ease of carrying. Remember—*small* bags are better. They won't tempt you to take more than you need.

What to take?

Your personal style, anticipated climate, and the kind of trip you plan will certainly influence what you take. A few general recommendations include:

- Dress in layers. Weather can be changeable, and layers take up less room than one bulky sweater or coat.

- Coordinate colors. Being able to mix and match pants, shirts, blouses, skirts, and scarves means taking much less while allowing for variety. Dark colors and prints are the best choice, since they show less soiling, and if you're hand-washing, dark colors dry faster in the sun.

- Cotton/polyester/rayon blends are the best travelers, though lightweight wool is a close second. Blends wash and dry faster and wool can easily be steamed free of wrinkles while you shower. Avoid garments made of 100 percent polyester, which can be uncomfortably hot and sticky in the summer.

- Women should avoid shoes with pointed or small heels, which easily get caught in cobblestones and rough streets.

- There is no need to take large quantities of shampoo, toothpaste, etc., as it is available everywhere.

- Sample sizes of shaving cream, toothpaste, shampoo, etc. are available in most large drugstores and are perfect for short trips.

- Resealable plastic bags, such as Ziploc®, are a wonderful addition to the traveler's suitcase and can be used to store cosmetics, bathroom supplies,

Tip: *Whenever possible hang washed clothing to dry while it is soaking wet—do not wring clothes out. The weight of the water will "iron" them when you smooth them out properly. A pants hanger attached to the bottom of a garment adds weight and helps to pull out wrinkles.*

vitamins, and medications. Nylons stay protected in bags, folded scarves stay neat, costume jewelry stays together. Wet bathing suits, washcloths, and clothes that may not have dried overnight are all good candidates for plastic bags, so take a few empties in various sizes.

- If you're pushed for space, try rolling your garments and securing them with rubber bands. One experienced traveler we know swears by this method.

- Always tape anything that might spill and pack it in a plastic bag (liquids expand at high altitudes).

- Carry the following items on your person, or pack them in your carry-on, *not in checked luggage:* passports, traveler's checks, credit cards, driver's license, addresses and phone numbers you may need on arrival, continuing tickets, Eurail or other train passes, car lease/rental papers, medical prescriptions and copies of prescriptions, a spare pair of eyeglasses or contact lenses if required, insurance forms and company phone numbers, and an inventory of what's in your checked baggage. Some people also carry overnight supplies and extra clothes in case bags turn up missing.

- Other items to include—these can be in checked bags—are your travel notebook, maps, guidebooks, other reading material, address book, camping carnet if you have one, Swiss army or other pocket knife (invaluable), and gifts for European friends. It's nice to take photographs from home, too, because the people you meet will be curious about America and your life here. Include photos of family members, your house, neighborhood, and the surrounding countryside. Postcards of your town, county, and state are also fun to share.

- Finally, put luggage tags on everything you are carrying, including cameras and luggage cart. Make sure you put your name and destination address on the inside of your bag, as well as the outside.

Typical warm-weather wardrobes

The following wardrobe suggestions are offered only as guidelines, as personal styles differ. Europeans generally dress conservatively; you will probably be more comfortable if you do the same. You will also be less conspicuously a tourist. (For instance, European men are seldom seen in shorts unless they're at the beach or on holiday.)

Men:

- ___ One pair of jeans
- ___ One pair of slacks of cotton/poly blend or lightweight wool. Good khaki pants can be dressed up or down and are suitable most everywhere.
- ___ One or two pair shorts that can double as swimsuit.
- ___ Four t-shirts/underwear/four pair socks
- ___ Two short-sleeve sport shirts
- ___ One long-sleeve dress shirt
- ___ One pair of casual shoes or sandals
- ___ One pair of comfortable dress shoes
- ___ Windbreaker, or wool pullover-sweater, or blazer
- ___ Warmups (sweats); a nice option, especially if camping
- ___ Raingear, especially if camping

Women:

- ___ One pair of walking shorts (not short shorts, please)
- ___ One or two skirts, patterned, not plain, preferably with deep pockets
- ___ One sleeveless sun dress—can be worn with t-shirt or turtleneck in cooler weather—or one dress that can become "formal" with appropriate accessories, depending on your style and preference—but not both.
- ___ One pair of washable slacks or jeans
- ___ One long-sleeved blouse; one short-sleeved blouse
- ___ One turtleneck; two short-sleeved t-shirts
- ___ One swimsuit
- ___ Six pairs of underwear, two bras (cotton is best in hot weather)
- ___ Two to four pairs of socks; one pair nylons or pantyhose
- ___ One pair of comfortable walking shoes (low or no heels)
- ___ One pair of dressier shoes (remember, small heels catch easily in uneven streets and cobblestones)
- ___ Windbreaker, pullover sweater, jacket or blazer
- ___ Warm-ups (sweats); a nice option, especially if camping
- ___ Raingear, especially if camping

Baggage regulations

Listed below are current international regulations. Because the airlines have the right to change these regulations, and because some are more strict than others, we recommend that you *confirm this information with your carrier(s)*. We recently tried carrying on board a bag that we have always carried and were told, "it will have to be checked" because it weighed over five kilos (11 lbs.). This necessitated a frantic repacking of some items and the quick purchase of a shopping bag to carry with us. (Some lessons don't seem to sink in.)

- Baggage allowances for international flights are more strictly enforced than for domestic flights. Total dimensions for each *checked* bag are 102 inches (measure length + width + height).

- No single bag can weigh more than 70 pounds.

- Regulations limit passengers to one carry-on, but you may also take a purse, camera bag, umbrella, and duty-free shopping bag. Remember that some airlines are more strict than others, and every one is different. We cannot stress this too much—*call first to see what the limits are.*

- Approved measurements for *carry-on* bags vary from 40–45 inches (length + width + height). Most airlines won't stop you from boarding if your bag is slightly larger, but it *must* fit under the seat or in the overhead compartment during take-off and landing, and it's your leg room you're losing.

Intra-Europe airlines have *different* regulations. Their weight allowances range from 22 to 66 pounds per person, depending on the place and class of ticket. Check with the airline or your travel agent for regulations, and then be sure you meet the *minimum* standards you plan to encounter throughout your trip. Excess baggage charges can be assessed for each piece of oversize or overweight luggage. (Our daughter once paid $75 for a single extra bag.)

Airlines ask that you remove any hooks or pullstraps on your baggage, and recommend that you lock bags. You may not carry restricted items, which include but are not limited to matches, lighter fluid, flammable solids/liquids, compressed gasses, and briefcases or attaché cases equipped with alarms.

Atlantic transit

Few people cross the Atlantic on ships these days, so we're addressing our transit suggestions to the great majority who fly. In our opinion there's no way to make flying—especially in coach class—pleasant, but there are steps you can take to make it less awful.

- Get your seat assignments early. If you plan to sleep, avoid getting seats near the galley or the bathrooms, where traffic is continuous, or directly in front of movie screens. Other seats to avoid are in the rows in front of emergency exits, which for safety reasons often have seats that don't tilt fully back. Seats directly behind bulkheads do have more leg room. However, there is no seat under which to stow your bag, and lack of tray tables in some planes can make dining awkward.

Tip: *Many U.S. airlines have banned passenger use of electronic devices such as AM-FM radios, cellular phones, CD players, TVs, remote-controlled toys, some computer peripherals, and more. Check with your carrier if you plan to use an electronic device in flight.*

- Wear loose-fitting clothing and get up and walk around the plane several times during the flight.

- Ear plugs, sleeping masks, and inflatable neck pillows make sleeping and relaxing easier.

- Most airlines offer special dietary meals, including vegetarian, kosher, diabetic, etc. We find these meals better than the standard fare; you don't have to be a vegetarian to order like one.

- Keep alcohol to a minimum; it increases jet lag and is dehydrating. We recommend the Argonne anti-jet-lag diet, which you'll find on page 98. Whether you use this diet or not, try to stay awake at your destination until a normal bedtime hour. Spend as much time as you can outside—the daylight helps your internal clock to adjust. Avoid napping and eating at odd times; try to fit into the new time schedule as quickly as possible. It's best to plan a light schedule for the first few days after arrival.

Arrival

First-time travelers are often jittery on arrival, wondering what to expect and sure they won't understand anything. Relax. International airports are well marked with signs in many languages, including English, as well as international icons. Take your time and don't panic; you will find everything you need.

Directions to trains and buses from airports to town are well marked in major airports. Your travel agent should be able to give you ground transportation information before you leave home, or check books like *From The Airport to the City* (Houghton Mifflin, 1992) or the *1995 Airport Transit Guide* (Salk International Travel Premiums) for the quickest and least expensive way to reach the city.

Remember that everywhere in Europe—airports, train stations, city centers—you will find information desks or offices marked with a small letter **i**. These are great sources of information for the weary traveler. They can help you find accommodations and money exchange offices, arrange day tours, and provide you with brochures of the area.

Here are some icons you might typically see in airports or train stations.

baby changing station | telephone | coffee shop | no smoking | restrooms | shower facilities

What if your bags aren't there when you are?

On exactly half of our trips a bag has been lost. If you're prepared, it needn't be a disaster. Here are a few tips to ease you through that mishap:

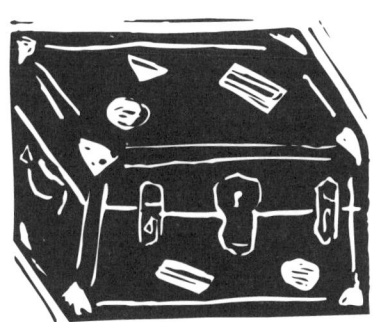

- As soon as you determine the bag is missing, seek out the nearest airline or baggage-area employee and report the loss. You will be tired and upset, but try to be patient. Thoughtfully and completely fill out all the forms you are given. Remember that the employees are trying to help you; anger will only worsen the situation.

- You will need to provide a complete, accurate description of your bag: size, color, and other characteristics. (We tie pieces of rainbow-colored luggage straps to our bags to distinguish them from others. If you *really* want to be prepared, carry a snapshot of your baggage to attach to the airline form.)

- Destination information. The airline will need the name of your hotel and other addresses on your itinerary, if you have them. Placing your name and address (home *and* destination) inside and outside the baggage doubles your chances of having the bag returned. Each time you move, change the destination address on your luggage tag and inside the bag. You don't want your bag returned home with three weeks remaining in your trip.

- Ask airline personnel for copies of any forms you give them. Ask for a telephone number to call to obtain information about your bag, or so that you can relay any change in your plans to the airline.

- An inventory of your bag will help if you need to file an insurance claim for loss. Some credit cards and baggage insurance policies provide for replacement kits or emergency purchases, so have your insurer's telephone number or credit card reporting number handy in your carry-on bag.

- Many airlines provide complimentary overnight kits containing toothbrushes and toothpaste, razors, shampoo, etc. If you need these things, be sure to ask for them.

Usually, your bag will be delivered to you within 24 hours. If your schedule forces you to move on ahead of your bag, be sure to let the airline know. It may take awhile to catch up with you, but it almost always does. On a recent trip, two men from Kargo Ekspress cheerfully delivered our bag in Bodrum—three days and 560 miles after our arrival in Istanbul.

Staying in touch while in Europe

Unless your trip is a long one you probably won't be receiving mail from home. In the event, however, that others do want to reach you, they can do so in several ways.

- *Poste Restante.* This term is known and understood throughout Europe and is similar to our general delivery. Ask your correspondent to print your last name clearly in capital letters, since mail is filed by last name. Underlining the last name will also help retrieval. Mail will usually be held 30 days, and can be addressed in this manner to any city, town, or village. You simply go to the post office and ask if mail has been received for you. (It might help to show your name written out clearly in block letters.) Using a small town for your pickup point will make retrieving mail easier. You'll avoid the long lines in major city post offices.

- If you know the names of the hotels you will be staying in along your route, your correspondents can direct mail to you in care of the hotel, with the expected date of your arrival written on the outside of the envelope.

- American Express client mail. If you are an American Express card holder you may have mail sent to you in care of Amex offices. A phone call to 800-528-4800 (NYC 212-477-5700) will get you a booklet called the *American Express Traveler's Companion* that lists the addresses of all Amex overseas offices. Mail will be held for 30 days, or until a specified date written on the envelope (remind your correspondents that Europeans always put the day first, then the month and year; thus June 15, 1995 would be written 15/6/95)

Phoning home

European telephones present a challenge, since every country has its own unique system. Some public phones are coin operated, some—especially in airports—allow you to use credit cards, some use a kind of debit card, others use only tokens. A few have instructions printed clearly on them in several languages, others leave you to fend for yourself. The nice phones show you the time remaining on your call in smart digital numbers; the rude phones cut you off in mid-sentence.

European telephone systems are operated by their respective governments, and you will usually find public telephones if you look for PTT offices (Post-Telephone-Telegraph), often connected to a central post office. Such places may have phone booths and even an employee to help you place an overseas call, but this kind of personal service is rapidly disappearing. Since the word *telephone* is internationally known, public phone booths can be spotted by watching for a variant of that word—usually a phonetic spelling, such as *telefon* (except in Finland, where the word is *puhelin*).

You may, of course, place a call from a private home, or from a hotel. Hotels can and often do add outrageous service charges to their telephone calls, so before picking up the phone, ask what charges will be added to your bill.

To call from one European country to another, or to call the United States from Europe, you must dial the country's access code, followed by a city code or area code, followed by the telephone number you wish to reach. You can simplify this by calling your long-distance carrier before you leave home. Ask them to send you their overseas calling information. AT&T, Sprint, and MCI all have simple access numbers that you can use in Europe to place calls home, or to parties in Europe. For instance:

- AT&T USA Direct Service connects you directly to the U.S. from more than 120 countries, and your call will be billed to your AT&T Calling Card. AT&T World Connect service lets you make calls between more than 65 countries while overseas. For information call 800-331-1140, extension 746.

- Sprint Express offers an access number to a Sprint operator in the U.S. Calls can be billed to your Sprint FONCARD, local telephone company card, American Express ConnectPlus card, or Discover ValuePhone card, or you can call collect. For information, call 800-877-4646.

- MCI offers Call USA services which, like AT&T, permit you to use almost all phones and charge on the phone company's credit card. MCI will furnish a wallet-sized card with access numbers and instructions. For more information, call 800-888-0800.

Avoiding jet lag

When we were planning a trip in the mid-80s, our research turned up the Argonne Anti-Jet-Lag Diet. It was developed by Dr. Charles F. Ehret of the Argonne National Laboratory's Division of Biological and Medical Research as an application of his fundamental studies of the daily biological rhythms of animals. It helps travelers quickly adjust their bodies' internal clocks to new time zones, and we've used it consistently since our first trial run. It really does help. (We don't use it on return trips though, since the thought of one last good French, German, Greek, Spanish, or Italian meal is too appealing.)

The diet is reprinted below, or you can write for a free wallet-sized copy to Argonne National Laboratory, 9700 South Cass Avenue, Argonne, IL 60439.

The Anti-Jet-Lag Diet*

1. DETERMINE BREAKFAST TIME at destination on day of arrival.

2. FEAST-FAST-FEAST-FAST—Start four days before breakfast time in step 1. On day one, FEAST; eat heartily, with high-protein breakfast and lunch and a high-carbohydrate dinner. No coffee except between 3 and 5 p.m. On day two, FAST on light meals of salads, light soups, fruits, and juices. Again, no coffee except between 3 and 5 p.m. On day three, FEAST again. On day four, FAST; if you drink caffeinated beverages, take them in the morning when traveling west, or between 6 and 11 p.m. when traveling east.

3. BREAK THE FINAL FAST at destination breakfast time. No alcohol on the plane. If the flight is long enough, sleep until normal breakfast time at destination, *but no later.* Wake up and FEAST on a high-protein breakfast. Stay awake and active. Continue the day's meals according to mealtimes at the destination.

FEAST on high-protein breakfasts and lunches to stimulate the body's active cycle. Suitable meals include steak, eggs, hamburgers, high-protein cereals, green beans.

FEAST on high-carbohydrate suppers to stimulate sleep. They include spaghetti and other pastas (but no meatballs), crepes (but no meat filling), potatoes, other starchy vegetables, and sweet desserts.

FAST days help deplete the liver's store of carbohydrates and prepare the body's clock for resetting. Suitable foods include fruit, light soups, broths, skimpy salads, unbuttered toast, half-pieces of bread. Keep calories and carbohydrates to a minimum.

*Used with permission of the Argonne National Laboratory.

Step 9 / to do...

___ 1 Do you have your airline reservations? If not, now is the time to make them.

    ❐ Ask about seat assignments at the same time.

    ❐ Order special meals if wanted. (This can be done up to a few days before departure.)

___ 2 Check with carrier regarding luggage restrictions. Remember to check every carrier—intraEurope flights often have tighter restrictions.

Maximum number of pieces allowed on most restrictive carrier you will use: _____

Maximum size carry-on bag allowed: _____ x _____ x _____
                                         width height length
Weight: _____

Maximum checked bag size allowed: _____ x _____ x _____
                                             width height length
Weight: _____

___ 3 Test pack your bag(s), including any carry-ons (purses, camera bags, etc.). Carry bags several blocks and repack if necessary.

___ 4 Ask credit card company if baggage insurance is included in its coverage. If not, consider purchasing a separate baggage insurance policy. (See Step 8 for travel insurance companies.)

___ 5 Make sure every bag, purse, camera bag, has an identification tag firmly attached. Do not depend on the flimsy tags airlines provide at check-in counters. Purchase extra luggage tags if needed.

___ 6 Prepare itinerary to leave with friends and family.

___ 7 Purchase traveler's checks; pack small calculator for currency exchange.

___ 8 Mark date on calendar to begin anti-jet-lag diet.

Notes

Step 10—Retain your memories

No matter how much fun we have traveling, at some point most of us have to come home and get back to the business of "real life." One of the joys of a happy trip is reliving the experience in your mind. Over time, a good trip gets better and better. The bad times are forgotten—or turned into great stories—and the good times take on a rich patina. Never, you will swear, was life so good.

You can jog your memory (or jolt it back to reality) in a number of ways, the most obvious of which is photography.

Take a camera

Nearly everyone travels with a camera, and the small size and sophisticated electronics contained in today's cameras make it easy to capture just about anything on film. Even novice photographers can use a point-and-shoot camera to their advantage, taking home photos to spark memories years hence.

Here are a few tips on traveling with a camera.

- Take your film and spare batteries with you. Specialized batteries for sophisticated cameras may be hard to find. Film is more expensive in Europe than in the U.S., sometimes considerably more, and in some out-of-the-way places stock is not frequently replenished. Always check the date on film and batteries before purchasing.

- Carry your film in a lead-shielded bag, or hand-check it through airport security. You will no doubt be told that airport x-rays aren't harmful to film, and in most cases, that's true. However, x-rays have a cumulative effect, especially on high-speed film (400 ASA and higher). You may have to go through several security checks during your trip, and no one can guarantee how much or how little exposure your film will be given. Usually, security workers will agree to hand-check film, but be prepared to insist. Have your film ready for inspection in a Ziploc® or other small bag. If you're shooting 35 mm, removing it from the containers will speed checking. Note that film left in *checked* luggage is subject to higher doses of x-rays.

- Carry lens cleaning materials (lens cleaning solution, lens tissue and a dust brush) and use them frequently. Ziploc® bags are great for storing filters and cleaning materials.

- Keep your film in a cool place. Bury it deep inside your luggage, so your clothing can act as an insulator against the heat of the day.

- Consider having a roll of film developed midway through your journey to confirm that your camera is working properly. Better to find out then, than after you get home.

- If you will be traveling in out-of-the-way places, or third-world countries, consider taking a Polaroid camera. Instant pictures can be great icebreakers, and can even trigger mini-adventures. They also make nice gifts for those you meet along the way. Purchase your Polaroid film in this country.

- Be aware of cultural differences and sensitivities (don't, for instance, take flash photos during a candlelight church ceremony, as we once saw done). Some people are sensitive about having their photograph taken. This becomes especially important if you are traveling in third-world countries or anywhere religious or superstitious beliefs forbid such images. Don't be an ugly American.

- Don't forget to put an I.D. sticker or luggage tag on your camera.

If you are trying to make the decision between taking slides or prints, consider how they will be used. Slides can certainly be more impressive, if you are prepared to show them. However, if you want enlargements, the quality you will get from slides is not generally as good as that from negatives.

How seriously you take photography is a personal issue. Carrying extra lenses and tripods can be burdensome, but some find them worth the trouble. There are many books available on travel photography; a few are listed in the resources chapter.

Video cameras

Video cameras are increasingly popular, and sometimes the decision to purchase is made just before a big trip. If you do buy a new camera (video or still), practice before you leave home and know your equipment well. Carry an extra battery and tapes with you. Newer cameras operate at both 120 and 240 volts. If yours is 120 only, you will need a converter to charge the battery. Whether 120 or 240, you will need an adaptor plug to use European electricity. Both converters and adaptors can be found in travel stores or in the travel sections of department stores. Purchase these before you depart.

Because of the nature of taping, which can continue for many minutes at a time, video cameras are often seen by others as intrusive. We urge you, therefore, to be sensitive to the reactions of the strangers around you who may not wish to be part of your home movie.

Keep a journal

Not everyone likes keeping a journal, but we have found it invaluable for triggering memories. A travel journal needn't be an in-depth report of your trip, or of your emotional state. Even a "daybook" with notes on hotels, new friend's addresses, itinerary, prices, etc., can be very useful when you get home. It's also a great place to tuck those admission stubs and restaurant receipts that you'll want for record keeping or a scrapbook.

Take a micro tape recorder

High-quality tape recorders are now so small they fit into shirt pockets. We have traveled with a recorder for years and have, among other things, the sounds of Big Ben, Swiss cow bells, street entertainers, and a delightful conversation with a woman in Inverness, describing sightings of the Loch Ness monster. A tape recorder can work as a journal, too, and as a way to communicate with friends and family at home. Don't forget to pack extra batteries.

Purchase post cards

Some of the best photography you will see is on post cards. They're also one of the best buys: they're inexpensive, take up almost no room, fill in the gaps your camera misses, and go nicely into a trip scrapbook when you get home. Posters also make good keepsakes. If kept in a cardboard tube they take up little space, and framed at home they are constant and decorative reminders.

Souvenirs

The word souvenir has declined in value over the years. Too many plastic ashtrays, tinny Eiffel Towers, and tasteless t-shirts have given souvenirs a bad name. We protest. The *American Heritage Dictionary* says a souvenir is "something serving as a token of remembrance; memento." That means anything that recalls your trip is a souvenir: labels from wine bottles, receipts, admission stubs and programs, a piece of hand-crafted pottery, a flea-market find, a leather bag from Florence, even (gasp) a tinny Eiffel tower. Anything. Within limits, we think toting souvenirs home is an acceptable practice, and prefer things we can use or see daily—constant reminders of a good trip.

If you're traveling light, you won't have room to carry much, but you can always mail an irresistible item home. In many countries you can purchase shipping boxes from the local PTT (post-telephone-telegraph). In some places, they will even wrap your items for you.

A final note: since there are so many legitimate souvenirs to choose from there is, of course, *no excuse* for taking "chips" from ruins or anything else that doesn't rightly belong to you. Those aren't souvenirs, they are stolen goods and may get you into serious trouble.

Coming home

Travelers who've been out of the country for more than 48 hours are allowed to bring back $400 worth of goods exempt from duty and federal tax. You will be given a customs form to fill out on the flight back home. It's not necessary to list every item purchased, if you have less than $400 worth of goods. The next $1,000 worth will be taxed at a flat 10 per cent. (Duty cannot be paid with a credit card. You will need cash, a personal check, or a traveler's check). It's a good idea to keep sales slips and charge slips, since you may need them when filling out your customs declaration. Note that customs officials do not need a search warrant to examine your luggage.

To make your experience with U.S. Customs tolerable, we suggest that you read two pamphlets before you leave home. They are *Know Before You Go* and *Buyer Beware!*. The latter lists restrictions on wildlife or wildlife products that are not permitted in the U.S. Both are available from any U.S. Customs office or by writing the U.S. Customs Service Publications Office, 1302 Constitution Avenue N.W., Washington, DC 20029 or by calling 202-927-5580.

U.S. Agriculture Department regulations do not permit you to bring in flowers, fresh fruit, vegetables, meats, or cuttings of any size. Also forbidden are products made from endangered species, liquor-filled chocolates, all fresh pork products (unless canned), including salamis and sausages, and of course, illicit drugs.

You're on your way . . .

If you've followed all the steps in this book, and completed all the *to dos,* you are well on your way to a having a successful trip. You have probably amassed piles of brochures, books, and magazines. Undoubtedly, you have talked to friends and strangers about their trips. You have studied maps, changed your destination (many times), visited the library, examined your wardrobes, purchased things you won't need, read and talked about all those brochures, books, and magazines; saved your money, and daydreamed. It's all part of the fun. Now, because you persevered, your idea has become a plan, and your trip will soon be a reality.

We hope the travel bug bites you hard. There is nothing more rewarding than traveling with an open mind and an open itinerary. Travel well, learn from your mistakes, and send us a postcard (c/o Artha Press, P.O. Box 82722, Portland, OR 97282-2722).

Step 10 / to do...

___1 Check to see that your camera is in working order, with clean lenses and fresh batteries.

___2 Purchase film and spare batteries before you leave. Take more film than you think you will need; once you get home, you'll regret not having more photos.

___3 Check to see that your tape recorder is in working order. Purchase extra batteries and tapes.

___4 Pack a journal or small blank book.

___5 Review the publications *Know Before You Go* and *Buyer Beware*.

___6 If you are taking a video camera, make sure you carry a European plug. If your camera does not have dual-voltage capability, pack a converter.

Afterword

Because the world *is* getting smaller, because travel is easier and easier, we have mixed feelings about urging you out into the world. We know that one trip means you will probably take another and another. Hundreds of thousands of people are doing just that.

Travel, like everything else in life, has a dark side; tourism can be seen as a curse. It destroys native cultures, litters pristine beaches, and covers fragile environments with gross monuments to luxury. So why are we encouraging more?

Because we have seen that those who travel with an open mind return home wiser and more sensitive to the people and problems "out there." Foreigners become friends, national characteristics become keys to understanding, other beliefs create yet another angle from which to view a truth. We hope that you and other good travelers will become thoughtful participants in the conversations we all must have to protect our environment and our multispecies, multicultural world for future generations.

–Karen and Ray Gilden
Portland, Oregon
January, 1995

Notes

Resources

Helpful books

The following list contains all books referenced in the text, as well as a selection of others we consider interesting or helpful.

1995 Airport Transit Guide, Salk International Travel Premiums, P.O. Box 1388, Sunset Beach, CA 90742; Tel. 714-893-0812.

Ferguson, George and LaVerne, *1995–96 Europe by Rail* (19th edition), Globe Pequot, Old Saybrook, CT, 1995.

AA Guide to Camping and Caravaning in Britain. Published by the Auto Club of Britain, available through the British Tourist Authority and in some U.S. bookstores.

Axtell, Roger E., *Do's and Taboos Around the World*, John Wiley & Sons.

Barbour, Bill and Mary, *Trading Places* (a how-to on exchanges), Rutledge Hill Press, Nashville, TN, 37219. (To order, call 800-532-4918.)

Budget Lodging Guide, Campus Travel Service, 1994. (Call 800-525-6633 to order. Accommodations in college dormitories and more, from $15 per night.)

Cope, Bob and Claudette, *European Camping and Caravaning*, Drake Publishers, New York, 1974.

Davies, Miranda and Natania Jansz, eds. *Women Travel*, The Rough Guides, London, 1990.

Dawood, Richard, M.D., *Travelers Health: How to Stay Healthy All Over the World*, Random House, New York, 1993.

Endicott, M.L., *Vagabond Globetrotting: State of the Art*, Enchiridion International, Cullowhee, NC, rev. 1989.

Europa Camping and Caravaning, available from Recreational Equipment, Inc., P.O. Box C88125, Seattle, WA 98188; Tel. 800-426-4840.

From the Airport to the City, Houghton Mifflin Company, Boston, 11th ed., 1992.

Gilford, Judith, *The Packing Book: Secrets of the Carry-on Traveler,* Ten Speed Press, Berkeley, CA.

Graff, Marie Louis, *Culture Schock: Spain,* Graphic Arts Center Publishing, Portland, OR, 1993.

Harriman, Cynthia, *Take Your Kids to Europe,* Mason-Grant, Portsmouth, NH, 1991.

Harris, Robert W., *Gypsying after 40: A Guide to Adventure and Self Discovery,* John Muir Publications, Santa Fe, NM, 1987.

Holing, Dwight, *A Guide to Earthtrips: Nature Travel on a Fragile Planet,* Living Planet Press, Los Angeles, 1991.

Kimbrough, John, *Vacation Home Exchange and Hospitality Guide.* A guide to exchange organizations. Kimco Communications. (Call 209-275-0893 to order.)

Manston, Peter B., *Manston's Travel Key Europe,* Travel Keys, Sacramento, CA. Updated regularly.

McCartney, Susan, *Travel Photography: A Complete Guide to How to Shoot and Sell,* Allworth Press, New York, 1992.

Monaghan, Kelly, *The Insiders Guide to Air Courier Bargains: How to Travel Worldwide for Next to Nothing,* Intrepid Traveler, New York, 3rd edition, 1994. (Call 800-356-9315 to order.)

Rogers, Barbara Radcliffe and Stillman Rogers, *Exploring Europe by Boat,* Globe Pequot, Old Saybrook, CT, 1994.

Simony, Maggy (ed.), *The Traveler's Reading Guide: Ready-made Reading Lists for the Armchair Traveler,* Facts On File Publications, New York, 1987.

Steves, Rick, *Europe Through the Back Door* (8th edition), John Muir Publications, Santa Fe, NM, 1988.

Taylor, Sally Adamson, *Culture Shock: France,* Graphic Arts Center Publishing, Portland, OR, 1990.

Travel Photography, (ed.) Time Life Books, New York, 1972.

Wood, Katie and George McDonald, *Europe by Train,* Harper Collins, New York, 1994.

Additional recommended reading

Daiches, David and John Flower, eds. *Literary Landscapes of the British Isles: A Narrative Atlas,* Paddington Press Ltd., New York, 1979. As the title suggests, this is a guide to writers' England: Hardy's Wessex, the Lake poets, Chaucer's world, Johnson's, Shakespeare's, Dickens, and Woolf's London, and more.

de Lampedusa, Giuseppe, *The Leopard,* Pantheon, 1960. Elegant novel of Sicilian aristocracy at the turn of the century.

Eco, Umberto, *The Name of the Rose:* Harcourt Brace Jovanovich, Inc., 1983. Murder and politics in 14th-century Italy.

Ford, Ford Madox, *Provence,* Ecco Press, Hopewell, New Jersey, 1979. Originally written in 1935, Graham Greene called it "an elaborate pattern of memories, historical and personal."

Massie, Suzanne, *Land of the Firebird: The Beauty of Old Russia,* Simon and Schuster, New York, 1980. A beautiful overview of prerevolutionary Russia, and a must for anyone planning a visit there.

Michener, James A., *Iberia: Spanish Travels and Reflections,* Random House, 1968. An excellent companion for anyone visiting Spain.

Orwell, George, *Down and Out in Paris and London,* Secker & Warbing, 1949. Two famous cities from a pauper's point of view.

Steinbeck, John, *The Acts of King Arthur and his Noble Knights,* Farrar, Straus and Giroux, 1976. This little-known version of the famous tales includes letters Steinbeck wrote to his editors—many from Europe—while researching the book, which was never completed.

Tuchman, Barbara W., *A Distant Mirror: The Calamitous 14th Century,* Alfred A. Knopf, New York, 1978. This history provides a rich backdrop for anyone traveling to Europe, and especially to France.

Young, Arthur, *Travels in France and Italy During the years 1787, 1788, and 1789,* Everyman's Library. An English agriculturalist reports on his travels during the French Revolution. Out of print, but worth searching for.

Other publications

Magazines

Affordable Travel. For subscription call 503-345-3800.

Conde Nast Traveler. For subscription call 800-777-0700.

EcoTraveler. For subscription call 800-344-8152.

International Travel News. For subscription call 916-457-3643.

National Geographic Traveler. For subscription call 800-638-4077 (TDD 800-548-9797).

Travel and Leisure. For subscription call 800-888-8728.

Newsletters

Best Fares Magazine
One-year subscription is $58, Tel. 800-635-3033.

Consumer Reports Travel Letter
P.O. Box 53629
Boulder, CO 80322
12 issues yearly; averages 24 pages; one-year subscription, $39.

France USA Contacts
104 West 14th Street,
New York, NY 10011.   Tel. 212-989-2929
Printed every two weeks with useful addresses and advertising for those planning to visit Paris. Includes apartments for rent, jobs, babysitting, etc. Single copies are $5, one-year subscription $55.

Inside Flyer
4715-C Town Center Drive
Colorado Springs, CO 80916
For frequent flyers. 12 issues yearly; averages 36 pages; one-year subscription, $33.

Out & About
542 Chapel Street
New Haven, CT 06511
Focus is gay and lesbian travelers. Ten issues yearly, averages 16 pages; one-year subscription is $49.

Passport Newsletter
350 W. Hubbard Street, Suite 440
Chicago, IL 60610
Concentrates on upscale destinations. 12 issues yearly, averages 20–24 pages, one-year subscription, $65.

Culturegrams

Brigham Young University
Kennedy Center Publications
P. O. Box 24538
Provo, UT 84602
To order (with a credit card) or to request an order form, call 801-378-6528.
Or send a stamped, self-addressed envelope to the address listed above.

U.S. Government publications

Order from Superintendent of Documents,
U.S. Government Printing Office, Washington, D.C. 20402
or tel. 202-512-1800:

>*Health Information for International Travelers ($7)*
>*Camper's First Aid ($2.50)*
>*Travel Tips for Older Americans*
>*Visa Requirements for Foreign Governments*
>*Your Trip Abroad*

Order from U.S. Customs Service (all are free),
1301 Constitution Avenue, N.W., Washington, D.C. 20229 or
tel. 202-927-5580:
>*Know Before You Go*
>*Buyer Beware*
>*Tips for Travelers*

Order from Superintendent of Documents,
Consumer Information Center, Department 133-B
Pueblo, Colorado 81009
>*Fly Rights*, a booklet explaining federal regulations in areas such as overbooking, smoking, refunds, passengers with disabilities, and health and comfort issues. Cost is $1.75 (check or money order).

Catalogs/bookstores

Book Passage
51 Tamal Vista Blvd.
Corte Madera, CA 94925   Tel. 800-999-7909

Forsyth Travel Library
9154 W. 57th Street (P.O. Box 2975)
Shawnee Mission, KS 66201-1375   Tel. 800-367-7984
A good source for maps and travel books of all kinds.

Magellan's
P.O. Box 5485
Santa Barbara, CA 93150-5485
Travel accessories.

Tel. 800-962-4943
Fax 805-568-5406

Traveller's Bookstore
22 West 52nd Street
New York, NY 10019
Tel. 212-664-0995
Send $2 for a catalog (free with purchase).

Europe Through the Back Door
P.O. Box 2009
Edmonds, WA 98020
Tel. 206-771-8303
Books and videos and travel accessories (no credit card orders accepted).

Organizations

American Youth Hostels Association
P.O. Box 37613
Washington, DC 20013-7613
Tel. 202-783-6161

CIEE International (Council for International Educational Exchange)
205 East 42nd Street
New York, NY 10017
Tel. 800-438-2643 or 212-661-1412

Family Campers and RVers
4804 Transit Road, Building 2
Depew, NY 14043-4704
Tel. 716-668-6242
International camping carnets and information about camping (formerly National Camper's and Hikers Association).

Federation of National Representation of the Experiment in International Living
P.O. Box 595, Main Street
Putney, VT 05346
Tel. 802-387-4210.
One- to four-week homestays through partner organizations in 17 countries.

The Friendship Force
57 Forsyth Street, N.W., Suite 900
Atlanta, GA 30303
Tel. 404-522-9490
Fax 404-688-6148
A private nonprofit organization sponsoring citizen exchanges, "bringing people of the world together in friendship."

International Association of Air Travel Couriers (IAATC)
P.O. Box 1349
Lake Worth, FL 33460   Tel. 407-582-8320
Clearinghouse for courier-related matters. Call or write for membership information.

Royal Oak Foundation
285 West Broadway, Suite 400
New York, NY 10013   Tel. 800-913-6565
This is the American affiliate of the National Trust for England, Wales, and Northern Ireland. Membership provides discounts on admission to National Trust properties, and rental access to houses, flats, and cottages available through the National Trust.

TraveLearn
P.O. Box 315
Lakeville, PA 18438   Tel. 717-226-9114 or 800-235-9114
Works with more than 260 colleges and universities to provide learning vacations of varying duration.

World Learning
Kipling Road, P.O. Box 676
Brattleboro, VT 05302-0676
Sponsors of the School for International Training, citizen exchange and language programs, au-pair homestays, and Elderhostel.

On the information superhighway

Among the growing number of organizations providing on-line travel services, including the ability to book hotels and purchase airline tickets, are Compuserve, Prodigy, and America Online. These companies charge a fee for their services.

If you have direct access to the Internet, you will find new travel resources every day through the World Wide Web (WWW). Here are two worth checking; they will undoutedly lead you to others:

- PCTravel (http://www.nando.net/pctravel.html): provides travelers with access to the Apollo Reservation system. You may use a credit card to establish a free account, check schedules, and order tickets, which are sent overnight at no extra charge.

- The Travel Resource Center at GNN, the Global Network Navigator, is a form of electronic magazine with extensive travel information. (http://nearnet.gnn.com/gnn/meta/travel/index.html).

Usenet groups, found on the Internet, that focus on travel are rec.travel.misc, rec.travel.marketplace, rec.travel.air, rec.travel.europe. To reach the rec.travel archives, which include travelogues, guides, and answers to frequently asked questions (FAQs), ftp to cc.umanitoba.ca:/rec-travel. For eco-travel information, you can ftp to igc.apc.org:/pub/green.travel.

Usenet groups discussing the culture and current events of nearly every country on earth are also found on the Internet, with the prefix "alt.culture" (alt.culture.france, alt.culture.italy, alt.culture.spain, etc.) Reading these "news" groups, which include opinions and comments from people around the globe, can provide insight about a country's culture, politics, and current events, before you arrive.

The U.S. State Department's Consular Affairs electronic bulletin board at 202-647-9225, provides consular information sheets, information on specific regions, and passport and visa information. Government-related Internet sites containing travel-related material include:
- World Tourism Organization—kraus.com
- U.S. State Department Travel Advisories—stolaf.edu
- U.S. Government gophers—ace.esusda.gov

Transportation companies

Major airlines to Europe:

American Airlines	Tel. 800-624-6262
Air Canada	Tel. 800-488-1800
Air France	Tel. 800-237-2747
Aer Lingus (Ireland)	Tel. 800-223-6537
Alitalia	Tel. 800-223-5730
Austrian Airlines	Tel. 800-843-0002
British Airways	Tel. 800-247-9297
Continental	Tel. 800-231-0856
Delta Air Lines	Tel. 800-221-1212
KLM Royal Dutch Airlines	Tel. 800-374-7747
Lufthansa German Airlines	Tel. 800-645-3880
Northwest Airlines	Tel. 800-447-4747
Sabena Belgian World Airlines	Tel. 800-955-2000
Scandinavian Airlines	Tel. 800-221-2350
Swissair	Tel. 800-221-4750
TAP Air Portugal	Tel. 800-247-8686
Trans World Airlines	Tel. 800-221-2000
United Airlines	Tel. 800-241-6522
Continental Airlines	Tel. 800-525-0280

Automobile rental/lease companies

Alamo Rent-a-Car	Tel. 800-327-9633
Auto Europe	Tel. 800-223-5555
Auto France (Peugeot)	Tel. 800-572-9655
Avis Rent-a-Car	Tel. 800-331-2112
Europe by Car	Tel. 800-223-1516
Foremost Euro-Car	Tel. 800-423-3111
Hertz Rent-a-Car	Tel. 800-654-3131
Kemwel Group	Tel. 800-678-0678
Renault European Delivery Service	Tel. 800-221-1052

Shipping and cruise companies

Abercrombie & Kent International	Tel. 800-323-7308
Cruise Company of Greenwich	Tel. 800-825-0826
Cunard	Tel. 800-221-4770
Europe Cruise Line	Tel. 800-688-3876
European Waterways	Tel. 800-922-0291
French Country Waterways, Ltd.	Tel. 800-222-1236
Julia Hoyt Canal Cruises	Tel. 800-852-2625
K.D. River Cruises of Europe	Tel. 800-858-8587
Premier Selections	Tel. 800-234-4000
OdessAmerica Cruise Company	Tel. 800-221-3254

Home exchange & rental organizations

Interhome USA, 124 Little Falls Road, Fairfield, NJ 07004; Tel. 201-882-6864, Fax 201-808-1742.

Intervac U.S., P.O. Box 590504, San Francisco, CA 94159; Tel. 415-435-3497 or 800-756-4663, Fax 415-435-7440.

The Invented City, 41 Sutter Street, Suite 1090, San Francisco, CA 94404; Tel. 415-673-6909 or 800-788-2489.

Loan-a-Home, 2 Park Lane, Apartment 6E, Mt. Vernon, NY 10552-3443; Tel. 914-664-7640.

Vacation Homes Unlimited, 18547 Soledad Canyon Road, Suite 223, Santa Clarita, CA 91351; Tel 805-298-0376 or 800-848-7927.

Vacation Exchange Club, P.O. Box 650, Key West, FL 33041; Tel. 800-638-3841, Fax 305-294-1448.

Europe

Clothing Conversion Charts
(Clothing will vary from country to country. Use this chart as a rough guide.)

Women

	Dresses/Suits						
American	8	10	12	14	16	18	20
British	30	32	34	36	38	40	42
Continental	36	38	40	42	44	46	48

	Stockings						Shoes			
American	8	8½	9	9½	10	10½	6	7	8	9
British/Continental	0	1	2	3	4	5	37	38	40	41

Men

	Suits/Overcoats						Shirts			
American	36	38	40	42	44	46	15	16	17	18
British/Continental	46	48	50	52	54	56	38	41	43	45

	Shoes								
American	5	6	7	8	8½	9	9½	10	11
British/Continental	38	39	41	42	43	43	44	44	45

Temperature conversion

To covert Fahrenheit into Centigrade, subtract 32 from the Fahrenheit figure and divide by 1.8.

To change from Centigrade into Fahrenheit, multiple Centigrade figure by 1.8 and add 32.

To change inches into centimetres, multiple by 2.54.
To change centimetres into inches, multiple by .39.

Measurement conversion

One mile = 1.609 kilometres (km.)
One kilometre = 0.62 miles

km:	10	20	30	40	50	60	70	80	90	100
Miles	6	12	19	25	31	37	44	50	56	62

Typical road signs

 No entry
 No parking
 No passing
 Height limit

 Width limit
 Speed limit in kph
 Traffic circle
 Bumpy road

 Yield
 Road narrows
 Bend in road
 Slippery

 End of restriction
 Hill
 Tunnel
 Pedestrian crossing

 Camping
 Information
 Parking
 Gas station

 Picnic area
 Mechanic
 Dining
 Hiking trail

Notes

Other reading

Things to buy

Packing list

Addresses

Itinerary

Index

A

A Safe Trip Abroad 86
AAA 33, 50
Advisories
　Department of Transportation 86
　U.S. State Department 86
airports 28
　airport security 78
America Online 16, 115
American Express 33, 34, 45
　Global Assist 83
　mail service 34, 96
American Youth Hostels 60, 114
apartments 60
Argonne Anti-Jet-Lag Diet 98
ATM machines 33, 34
autobahn 48, 50
automobiles
　auto flea market 49
　expense of 31
　insurance (CDW) 52
　rental/lease agencies 52
　travel by 48

B

Baedecker's 15
baggage
　insurance 85, 92, 95
　lost 95
Baltic Rail Card 46
Berkeley Guides 14
Better Business Bureau 61
Blue Guides 15
boat & cruise company listings 54, 117
British National Trust 31
Britrail 45, 46

C

cameras 101
Camper's First Aid 86, 113
campgrounds 4, 63
　conditions 63
camping
　by car 48
　equipment 28, 63, 64
Center for Disease Control 82

changing money 32, 36
children, traveling with 5
Chunnel 28
Collision Damage Waiver (CDW) 52
commissions 28, 32, 33
Compuserve 16, 115
computer resources 43
Consular Affairs Bulletin Board 86
Council for International Education Exchange 29, 114
credit cards 31, 33, 34, 49, 52, 77, 83
  protecting 80
cruises 53
Culturegrams 15, 18, 113
currency 33
Czech Flexipass 47

D

daily budget 26
dental care 82
diarrhea 82
Diner's Club International 34
dollars 32
driving record 49

E

EcoTraveler 15
Elderhostel 62
emergencies 29
emergency medical evacuation 85
English language 39, 94
Eurail 17, 25, 26, 31, 43, 45
Europa Camping and Caravaning Guide 64, 109
Europass. *See* Eurail
Europe Through the Back Door 14, 110
European East Pass 47
exchange rate 15, 32
expenses 25
  food 29
  lodging 28
  planning for 28
  sightseeing 29

F

Family Campers & RVers Assoc. 65, 114
Federation of National Representation of the Experiment in International Living 62, 114
ferries 17, 54
  cost of 28
Fielding's
  Fielding's City Fax 14
film 101

protecting 101
Flexipass 44, 46. *See also* Eurail
Fodor's 14, 26, 59
   Fodor's World View Travel Update 14
foreign currency. *See* changing money
foreign language skills 39
France Rail pass 46
French National Railways 45
Friendship Force, The 114
From the Airport to the City, 28, 94, 109
Frommer's 14, 26, 59

G

gasoline 28
   cost of 49
German Rail pass 47
green card 50, 78. *See* automobiles: insurance

H

health care 81
Health Information for International Travelers 16, 86, 113
homestays 62
hotels 59, 79
house exchanges 61
   listings 117
How to Camp Europe by Train 64
Hungarian Flexipass 47

I

illness 81
information desks 94
insurance
   accident 84
   baggage 83, 85
   flight 85
   medical 84
   travel 17, 83
   trip cancellation 50, 84
Interhome USA 62
International Association for Medical Assistance 83
International Association of Air Travel Couriers 115
International Camping Carnet 65
International Driving Permit 50
International Herald Tribune 49
Internet 115
Intervac U.S. 62
itinerary 5

J

jet lag. *See* Argonne Anti-Jet-Lag Diet

K

Know Before You Go 16, 104

L

laundromats 64
Let's Go 14, 26, 59
Loan-a-Home 62
Lonely Planet 14, 26, 59
luggage
  protecting 78
luggage cart 89

M

magazines 15
MasterCard 33, 34
medical help 83
  referrals 83
Michelin Camping Guide 64
Michelin Green Guides 15
money
  cutting costs 29
  estimating costs 25
money exchange offices 32, 94

N

National tourist offices 31, 54, 59
  directory of 20

P

packing 89
passport 69, 77, 78
  passport services 69
  photos 69, 73, 80
  protecting 78
photocopies 80
photography 101
PIN (personal identification number) 32
police report 79
Polrailpass 47
Poste Restante 96
prescription drugs 81
Prodigy 16, 115
PTT offices 96
purchase/repurchase. *See* automobiles: rental/lease agencies

R

Rail 'N Drive 45, 46, 47
rail passes, summary of 45
Recreational Equipment, Inc. 64

road maps 55
Royal Oak Foundation 115. *See also* British National Trust

S

safety 77
Saverpass 44, 46. *See also* Eurail
Scanrail Pass 47
self-defense 81
shoulder seasons 4
Spain Flexipass 47
street vendors 30
suitcase. *See* luggage
Swiss Flexipass 47

T

Take Your Kids to Europe 6, 110
telephones 96
The Friendship Force 62
The Invented City 62
thieves 77, 79
Thomas Cook 33
transportation 25, 43
   air travel 43, 116
   automobile 48, 117
   rail 43
travel advisories, U.S. Dept. of Transportation 86
travel agents 16, 43, 59
Travel Tips for Older Americans 86, 113
TraveLearn 115
traveler's checks 33, 77
   protecting 80
Travelers Health: How to Stay Healthy All Over the World 83
Traveller's Bookstore 18

U

U. S. Customs 104
U.S. Agriculture Department 104
U.S. Department of Health and Human Services 82
U.S. Department of State 116. *See* passport
   advisories 86
U.S. Government Publications 16
   Buyer Beware 16, 104, 113
   Camper's First Aid 16
   Fly Rights 113
   Know Before You Go 113
   Tips for Travelers 16, 113
   Visa Requirements for Foreign Governments 16
   Your Trip Abroad 16, 86
U.S. Servas 63
Usenet 16, 116

V

Vacation Exchange Club 62
Vacation Homes Unlimited 62
valuables, protecting 79
value added tax (VAT) 35, 44, 48, 49
video cameras 102
Visa card 33
Visa Requirements for Foreign Governments 113
visa service 70
visas 70

W

wardrobe suggestions 91
women traveling alone 80
World Learning 115
World Wide Web (WWW) 115

Y

Your Trip Abroad 113
Youth Flexipass 46. *See also* Eurail
youth hostels 60

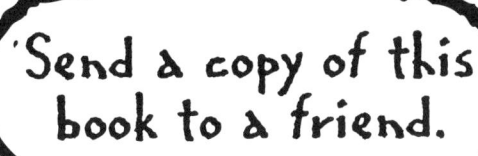

How to Plan Your Trip to Europe makes a great gift. Books are $14.95 each plus $2.50 for shipping and handling. Just mail this form, with your check or money order, to:

    Artha Press
    P.O. Box 82722
    Portland, OR 97282-2722

For VISA, Mastercard, or American Express orders, call 1-800-858-9055.

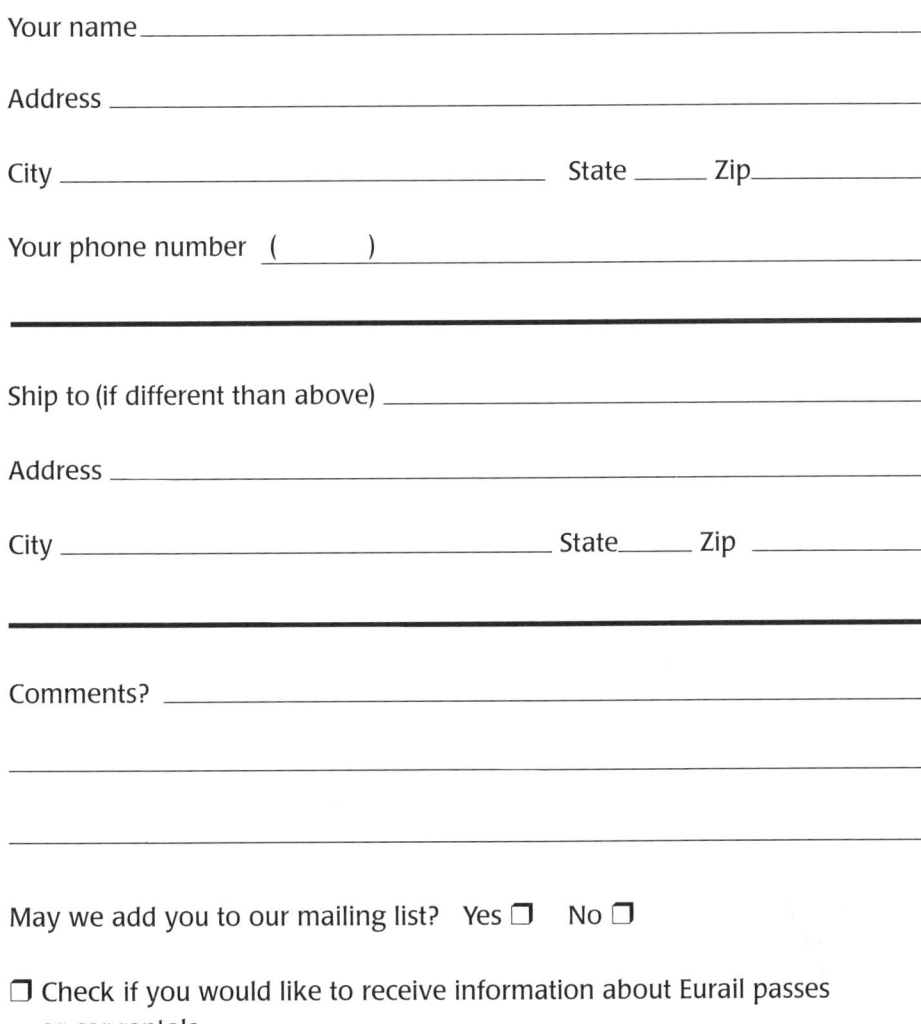

Your name _____

Address _____

City _____ State _____ Zip _____

Your phone number (_____) _____

Ship to (if different than above) _____

Address _____

City _____ State _____ Zip _____

Comments? _____

_____

_____

May we add you to our mailing list? Yes ❏   No ❏

❏ Check if you would like to receive information about Eurail passes or car rentals.